BY BILLY COLLINS

Aimless Love: New and Selected Poems
Horoscopes for the Dead
Ballistics
The Trouble with Poetry and Other Poems
Nine Horses
Sailing Alone Around the Room: New and Selected Poems
Picnic, Lightning
The Art of Drowning
Questions About Angels
The Apple That Astonished Paris

EDITED BY BILLY COLLINS

Bright Wings: An Illustrated Anthology of Poems About Birds
(illustrations by David Allen Sibley)
180 More: Extraordinary Poems for Every Day
Poetry 180: A Turning Back to Poetry

AIMLESS LOVE

AIMLESS LOVE

New and Selected Poems

Billy Collins

RANDOM HOUSE
NEW YORK

Published in the United States by Random House,
an imprint of The Random House Publishing Group,
a division of Random House, Inc., New York.

RANDOM HOUSE and the HOUSE colophon are registered
trademarks of Random House, Inc.

ISBN 978-0-679-64405-7
eBook ISBN 978-0-8129-8465-1

Printed in the United States of America on acid-free paper

www.atrandom.com

4 6 8 9 7 5 3

Book design by Dana Leigh Blanchette
Title-page and part-title photograph: © iStockphoto.com

To all the editors who have ushered
my poems into print, especially
David Ebershoff
Daniel Menaker
Ed Ochester
Joseph Parisi
Don Paterson
Miller Williams

Little soul
little stray
little drifter
now where will you stay
all pale and all alone
after the way
you used to make fun of things?

—Hadrian

CONTENTS

FROM *THE TROUBLE WITH POETRY*

(2005)

FROM *HOROSCOPES FOR THE DEAD*

(2011)

NEW POEMS

Reader

Looker, gazer, skimmer, skipper,
thumb-licking page turner, peruser,
you getting your print-fix for the day,
pencil-chewer, note taker, marginalianist
with your checks and X's
first-timer or revisiter,
browser, speedster, English major,
flight-ready girl, melancholy boy,
invisible companion, thief, blind date, perfect stranger—

that is me rushing to the window
to see if it's you passing under the shade trees
with a baby carriage or a dog on a leash,
me picking up the phone
to imagine your unimaginable number,
me standing by a map of the world
wondering where you are—
alone on a bench in a train station
or falling asleep, the book sliding to the floor.

FROM *NINE HORSES*
(2002)

The Country

I wondered about you
when you told me never to leave
a box of wooden, strike-anywhere matches
lying around the house because the mice

might get into them and start a fire.
But your face was absolutely straight
when you twisted the lid down on the round tin
where the matches, you said, are always stowed.

Who could sleep that night?
Who could whisk away the thought
of the one unlikely mouse
padding along a cold water pipe

behind the floral wallpaper
gripping a single wooden match
between the needles of his teeth?
Who could not see him rounding a corner,

the blue tip scratching against a rough-hewn beam,
the sudden flare, and the creature
for one bright, shining moment
suddenly thrust ahead of his time—

now a fire-starter, now a torch-bearer
in a forgotten ritual, little brown druid
illuminating some ancient night.
Who could fail to notice,

lit up in the blazing insulation,
the tiny looks of wonderment on the faces
of his fellow mice, one-time inhabitants
of what once was your house in the country?

Velocity

In the club car that morning I had my notebook
open on my lap and my pen uncapped,
looking every inch the writer
right down to the little writer's frown on my face,

but there was nothing to write about
except life and death
and the low warning sound of the train whistle.

I did not want to write about the scenery
that was flashing past, cows spread over a pasture,
hay rolled up meticulously—
things you see once and will never see again.

But I kept my pen moving by drawing
over and over again
the face of a motorcyclist in profile—

for no reason I can think of—
a biker with sunglasses and a weak chin,
leaning forward, helmetless,
his long thin hair trailing behind him in the wind.

I also drew many lines to indicate speed,
to show the air becoming visible
as it broke over the biker's face

the way it was breaking over the face
of the locomotive that was pulling me
toward Omaha and whatever lay beyond Omaha
for me, all the other stops to make

before the time would arrive to stop for good.
We must always look at things
from the point of view of eternity,

the college theologians used to insist,
from which, I imagine, we would all
appear to have speed lines trailing behind us
as we rush along the road of the world,

as we rush down the long tunnel of time—
the biker, of course, drunk on the wind,
but also the man reading by a fire,

speed lines coming off his shoulders and his book,
and the woman standing on a beach
studying the curve of horizon,
even the child asleep on a summer night,

speed lines flying from the posters of her bed,
from the white tips of the pillow cases,
and from the edges of her perfectly motionless body.

"More Than a Woman"

Ever since I woke up today,
a song has been playing uncontrollably
in my head—a tape looping

over the spools of the brain,
a rosary in the hands of a frenetic nun,
mad fan belt of a tune.

It must have escaped from the radio
last night on the drive home
and tunneled while I slept

from my ears to the center of my cortex.
It is a song so cloying and vapid
I won't even bother mentioning the title,

but on it plays as if I were a turntable
covered with dancing children
and their spooky pantomimes,

as if everything I had ever learned
was being slowly replaced
by its slinky chords and the puff-balls of its lyrics.

It played while I watered the plants
and continued when I brought in the mail
and fanned out the letters on a table.

It repeated itself when I took a walk
and watched from a bridge
brown leaves floating in the channels of a current.

Late in the afternoon it seemed to fade,
but I heard it again at the restaurant
when I peered in at the lobsters

lying on the bottom of an illuminated
tank which was filled to the brim
with their copious tears.

And now at this dark window
in the middle of the night
I am beginning to think

I could be listening to music of the spheres,
the sound no one ever hears
because it has been playing forever,

only the spheres are colored pool balls,
and the music is oozing from a jukebox
whose lights I can just make out through the clouds.

Aimless Love

This morning as I walked along the lakeshore,
I fell in love with a wren
and later in the day with a mouse
the cat had dropped under the dining room table.

In the shadows of an autumn evening,
I fell for a seamstress
still at her machine in the tailor's window,
and later for a bowl of broth,
steam rising like smoke from a naval battle.

This is the best kind of love, I thought,
without recompense, without gifts,
or unkind words, without suspicion,
or silence on the telephone.

The love of the chestnut,
the jazz cap and one hand on the wheel.

No lust, no slam of the door—
the love of the miniature orange tree,
the clean white shirt, the hot evening shower,
the highway that cuts across Florida.

No waiting, no huffiness, or rancor—
just a twinge every now and then

for the wren who had built her nest
on a low branch overhanging the water
and for the dead mouse,
still dressed in its light brown suit.

But my heart is always propped up
in a field on its tripod,
ready for the next arrow.

After I carried the mouse by the tail
to a pile of leaves in the woods,
I found myself standing at the bathroom sink
gazing down affectionately at the soap,

so patient and soluble,
so at home in its pale green soap dish.
I could feel myself falling again
as I felt its turning in my wet hands
and caught the scent of lavender and stone.

Absence

This morning as low clouds
skidded over the spires of the city

I found next to a bench
in a park an ivory chess piece—

the white knight as it turned out—
and in the pigeon-ruffling wind

I wondered where all the others were,
lined up somewhere

on their red and black squares,
many of them feeling uneasy

about the salt shaker
that was taking his place,

and all of them secretly longing
for the moment

when the white horse
would reappear out of nowhere

and advance toward the board
with his distinctive motion,

stepping forward, then sideways
before advancing again,

the same moves I was making him do
over and over in the sunny field of my palm.

Royal Aristocrat

My old typewriter used to make so much noise
I had to put a cushion of newspaper
beneath it late at night
so as not to wake the whole house.

Even if I closed the study door
and typed a few words at a time—
the best way to work anyway—
the clatter of keys was still so loud

that the gray and yellow bird
would wince in its cage.
Some nights I could even see the moon
frowning down at me through the winter trees.

That was twenty years ago,
yet as I write this with my soft lead pencil
I can still hear that distinctive sound,
like small arms fire across a border,

one burst after another
as my wife turned in her sleep.
I was a single monkey
trying to type the opening lines of my Hamlet,

often doing nothing more
than ironing pieces of paper in the platen
then wrinkling them into balls
to flick into the wicker basket.

Still, at least I was making noise,
adding to the great secretarial din,
that chorus of clacking and bells,
thousands of desks receding into the past.

And that was more than can be said
for the mute rooms of furniture,
the speechless cruets of oil and vinegar,
and the tall silent hedges surrounding the house.

Such deep silence on those nights—
just the sound of my typing
and a few stars singing a song their mother
sang when they were mere babies in the sky.

Paris

In the apartment someone gave me,
the bathroom looked out on a little garden
at the bottom of an air shaft
with a few barely sprouting trees,
ivy clinging to the white cinder blocks,
a blue metal table and a rusted chair
where, it would seem, no one had ever sat.

Every morning, a noisy bird
would flutter down between the buildings,
perch on a thin branch and yell at me
in French bird-talk
while I soaked in the tub
under the light from the pale translucent ceiling.

And while he carried on, I would lie there
in the warm soapy water
wondering what shirt I would put on that day,
what zinc-covered bar I would stand at
with my *Herald-Tribune* and a cup of strong coffee.

After a lot of squawking, he would fly
back into the sky leaving only the sound
of a metal store-front being raised
or a scooter zipping by outside,
which was my signal

to stand up in the cloudy water
and reach for a towel,

time to start concentrating on which way
I would turn after I had locked the front door,
what shop signs I would see,
what bridges I would lean on
to watch the broad river undulating
like a long-playing record under the needle of my eye.

Time to stand dripping wet and wonder
about the hordes of people
I would pass in the street, mostly people
whose existence I did not believe in,
but a few whom I would glance at
and see my whole life
the way you see the ocean from the shore.

One morning after another,
I would fan myself dry with a towel
and wonder about what paintings
I would stand before that day,
looking forward to the usual—
the sumptuous reclining nudes,
the knife next to a wedge of cheese,
a landscape with pale blue mountains,
the heads and shoulders of gods
struggling with one another,
a foot crushing a snake—

but always hopeful for something new
like yesterday's white turkeys in a field
or the single stalk of asparagus on a plate
in a small gilded frame,

always ready, now that I am dressed,
to cheer the boats of the beautiful,
the boats of the strange,
as they float down the river of this momentous day.

Istanbul

It was a pleasure to enter by a side street
in the center of the city
a bathhouse said to be 300 years old,
old enough to have opened the pores of Florence Nightingale
and soaped the musical head of Franz Liszt.

And it was a pleasure to drink
cold wine by a low wood fire
before being directed to a small room in an upper gallery,
a room with a carpet and a narrow bed
where I folded my clothes into a pile
then came back down, naked
except for a gauzy striped cloth tucked around my waist.

It was an odd and eye-opening sensation
to be led by a man with close-cropped hair
and spaces between his teeth
into a steamy marble rotunda
and to lie there alone on the smooth marble
watching the droplets fall through the beams
of natural light in the high dome
and later to hear the song I sang—
"She Thinks I Still Care"—echo up into the ceiling.

I felt like the last of the sultans
when the man returned and began to scrub me—

to lather and douse me, scour and shampoo me,
and splash my drenched body
with fresh warm water scooped from a marble basin.

But it was not until he sudsed me
behind my ears and between my toes
that I felt myself filling with gratitude
the way a cloud fills with rain,
the way a glass pipe slowly fills with smoke.

In silence I thanked the man
who scrubbed the bottoms of my feet.
I thanked the history of the Turkish bath
and the long chain of bathmen standing unshaven,
arms folded, waiting for the next customer
to come through the swinging doors of frosted glass.

I thanked everyone whose job
it ever was to lay hands on the skin of strangers,
and I gave general thanks that I was lying
facedown in a warm puddle of soap
and not a warm puddle of blood
in some corner of this incomprehensible city.

As one bucket after another
of warm water was poured over my lowered head,
I stopped thinking of who and what to thank
and rode out on a boat of joy,
a blue boat of marble and soap,

rode out to the entrance of the harbor
where I raised a finger of good-bye
then felt the boat begin to rise and fall
as it met the roll of the incoming waves,
bearing my body, my clean, blessed body out to sea.

Love

The boy at the far end of the train car
kept looking behind him
as if he were afraid or expecting someone

and then she appeared in the glass door
of the forward car and he rose
and opened the door and let her in

and she entered the car carrying
a large black case
in the unmistakable shape of a cello.

She looked like an angel with a high forehead
and somber eyes and her hair
was tied up behind her neck with a black bow.

And because of all that,
he seemed a little awkward
in his happiness to see her,

whereas she was simply there,
perfectly existing as a creature
with a soft face who played the cello.

And the reason I am writing this
on the back of a manila envelope
now that they have left the train together

is to tell you that when she turned
to lift the large, delicate cello
onto the overhead rack,

I saw him looking up at her
and what she was doing
the way the eyes of saints are painted

when they are looking up at God
when he is doing something remarkable,
something that identifies him as God.

Obituaries

These are no pages for the young,
who are better off in one another's arms,

nor for those who just need to know
about the price of gold,
or a hurricane that is ripping up the Keys.

But eventually you may join
the crowd who turn here first to see
who has fallen in the night,
who has left a shape of air walking in their place.

Here is where the final cards are shown,
the age, the cause, the plaque of deeds,
and sometimes an odd scrap of news—
that she collected sugar bowls,
that he played solitaire without any clothes.

And all the survivors huddle at the end
under the roof of a paragraph
as if they had sidestepped the flame of death.

What better way to place a thin black frame
around the things of the morning—
the hand-painted cup,

the hemispheres of a cut orange,
the slant of sunlight on the table?

And sometimes a most peculiar pair turns up,
strange roommates lying there
side by side upon the page—
Arthur Godfrey next to Man Ray,
Ken Kesey by the side of Dale Evans.

It is enough to bring to mind an ark of death,
not the couples of the animal kingdom,
but rather pairs of men and women
ascending the gangplank two by two,

a surgeon and a model,
a balloonist and a metal worker,
an archeologist and an authority on pain.

Arm-in-arm, they get on board
then join the others leaning on the rails,
all saved at last from the awful flood of life—

so many of them every day
there would have to be many arks,
an armada to ferry the dead
over the heavy waters that roll beyond the world,

and many Noahs too,
bearded and fiercely browed, vigilant up there at every prow.

Today

If ever there were a spring day so perfect,
so uplifted by a warm intermittent breeze

that it made you want to throw
open all the windows in the house

and unlatch the door to the canary's cage,
indeed, rip the little door from its jamb,

a day when the cool brick paths
and the garden sprouting tulips

seemed so etched in sunlight
that you felt like taking

a hammer to the glass paperweight
on the living room end table,

releasing the inhabitants
from their snow-covered cottage

so they could walk out,
holding hands and squinting

into this larger dome of blue and white,
well, today is just that kind of day.

Creatures

Hamlet noticed them in the shapes of clouds,
but I saw them in the furniture of childhood,
creatures trapped under surfaces of wood,

one submerged in a polished sideboard,
one frowning from a chair-back,
another howling from my mother's silent bureau,
locked in the grain of maple, frozen in oak.

I would see these presences, too,
in a swirling pattern of wallpaper
or in the various greens of a porcelain lamp,
each looking so melancholy, so damned,
some peering out at me as if they knew
all the secrets of a secretive boy.

Many times I would be daydreaming
on the carpet and one would appear next to me,
the oversize nose, the hollow look.

So you will understand my reaction
this morning at the beach
when you opened your hand to show me
a stone you had picked up from the shoreline.

"Do you see the face?" you asked
as the cold surf circled our bare ankles.
"There's the eye and the line of the mouth,
like it's grimacing, like it's in pain."

"Well, maybe that's because it has a fissure
running down the length of its forehead
not to mention a kind of twisted beak," I said,

taking the thing from you and flinging it out
over the sparkle of blue waves
so it could live out its freakish existence
on the dark bottom of the sea

and stop bothering innocent beach-goers like us,
stop ruining everyone's summer.

Tipping Point

At home, the jazz station plays all day,
so sometimes it becomes indistinct,
like the sound of rain,
birds in the background, the surf of traffic.

But today I heard a voice announce
that Eric Dolphy, 36 when he died,
has now been dead for 36 years.

I wonder—
did anyone sense something
when another Eric Dolphy lifetime
was added to the span of his life,

when we all took another
full Dolphy step forward in time,
flipped over the Eric Dolphy yardstick once again?

It would have been so subtle—
like the sensation you might feel
as you passed through the moment

at the exact center of your life
or as you crossed the equator at night in a boat.

I never gave it another thought,
but could that have been the little shift
I sensed a while ago
as I walked down in the rain to get the mail?

Nine Horses

For my birthday,
my wife gave me nine horse heads,
ghostly photographs on squares of black marble,
nine squares set in one large square,
a thing so heavy that the artist himself
volunteered to hang it
from a wood beam against a white stone wall.

Pale heads of horses in profile
as if a flashcube had caught them walking in the night.

Pale horse heads
that overlook my reading chair,
the eyes so hollow they must be weeping,

the mouths so agape they could be dead—
the photographer standing over them
on a floor of straw, his black car parked by the stable door.

Nine white horses,
or one horse the camera has multiplied by nine.

It hardly matters, such sadness is gathered here
in their long white faces
so far from the pasture and the cube of sugar—
the face of St. Bartholomew, the face of St. Agnes.

Odd team of horses,
pulling nothing,
look down on these daily proceedings.

Look down upon this table and these glasses,
the furled napkins,
the evening wedding of the knife and fork.

Look down like a nine-headed god
and give us a sign of your displeasure
or your gentle forbearance
so that we may rejoice in the error of our ways.

Look down on this ring
of candles flickering under your pale heads.

Let your suffering eyes
and your anonymous deaths
be the bridle that keeps us from straying from each other

be the cinch that fastens us to the belly of each day

as it gallops away, hooves sparking into the night.

Litany

You are the bread and the knife,
The crystal goblet and the wine . . .

—Jacques Crickillon

You are the bread and the knife,
the crystal goblet and the wine.
You are the dew on the morning grass
and the burning wheel of the sun.
You are the white apron of the baker
and the marsh birds suddenly in flight.

However, you are not the wind in the orchard,
the plums on the counter,
or the house of cards.
And you are certainly not the pine-scented air.
There is no way you are the pine-scented air.

It is possible that you are the fish under the bridge,
maybe even the pigeon on the general's head,
but you are not even close
to being the field of cornflowers at dusk.

And a quick look in the mirror will show
that you are neither the boots in the corner
nor the boat asleep in its boathouse.

It might interest you to know,
speaking of the plentiful imagery of the world,
that I am the sound of rain on the roof.

I also happen to be the shooting star,
the evening paper blowing down an alley,
and the basket of chestnuts on the kitchen table.

I am also the moon in the trees
and the blind woman's tea cup.
But don't worry, I am not the bread and the knife.
You are still the bread and the knife.
You will always be the bread and the knife,
not to mention the crystal goblet and—somehow—the wine.

The Literary Life

I woke up this morning,
as the blues singers like to boast,
and the first thing to enter my mind,
as the dog was licking my face, was Coventry Patmore.

Who *was* Coventry Patmore?
I wondered, as I rose
and set out on my journey to the encyclopedia
passing some children and a bottle cap on the way.

Everything seemed more life-size than usual.
Light in the shape of windows
hung on the walls next to the paintings
of birds and horses, flowers and fish.

Coventry Patmore,
I'm coming to get you, I hissed,
as I entered the library like a man stepping
into a freight elevator of science and wisdom.

How many things have I looked up
in a lifetime of looking things up?
I wondered, as I set the book on the piano
and began turning its large, weightless pages.

How would the world look
if all of its things were neatly arranged
in alphabetical order? I wondered,
as I found the *P* section and began zeroing in.

How long before I would forget Coventry Patmore's
dates and the title of his long poem
on the sanctity of married love?
I asked myself as I closed the door to that room

and stood for a moment in the kitchen,
taking in the silvery toaster, the bowl of lemons,
and the white cat, looking as if
he had just finished his autobiography.

Writing in the Afterlife

I imagined the atmosphere would be clear,
shot with pristine light,
not this sulfurous haze,
the air ionized as before a thunderstorm.

Many have pictured a river here,
but no one mentioned all the boats,
their benches crowded with naked passengers,
each bent over a writing tablet.

I knew I would not always be a child
with a model train and a model tunnel,
and I knew I would not live forever,
jumping all day through the hoop of myself.

I had heard about the journey to the other side
and the clink of the final coin
in the leather purse of the man holding the oar,
but how could anyone have guessed

that as soon as we arrived
we would be asked to describe this place
and to include as much detail as possible—
not just the water, he insists,

rather the oily, fathomless, rat-happy water,
not simply the shackles, but the rusty,
iron, ankle-shredding shackles—
and that our next assignment would be

to jot down, off the tops of our heads,
our thoughts and feelings about being dead,
not really an assignment,
the man rotating the oar keeps telling us—

think of it more as an exercise, he groans,
think of writing as a process,
a never-ending, infernal process,
and now the boats have become jammed together,

bow against stern, stern locked to bow,
and not a thing is moving, only our diligent pens.

No Time

In a rush this weekday morning,
I tap the horn as I speed past the cemetery
where my parents lie buried
side by side under a smooth slab of granite.

Then, all day long, I think of him rising up
to give me that look
of knowing disapproval
while my mother calmly tells him to lie back down.

Elk River Falls

is where the Elk River falls
from a rocky and considerable height,
turning pale with trepidation at the lip
(it seemed from where I stood below)
before it unbuckles from itself
and plummets, shredded, through the air
into the shadows of a frigid pool,
so calm around the edges, a place
for water to recover from the shock
of falling apart and coming back together
before it picks up its song again,
goes sliding around some massive rocks
and past some islands overgrown with weeds
then flattens out, slips around a bend,
and continues on its winding course,
according to this camper's guide,
then joins the Clearwater at its northern fork
which leads it all to the distant sea
where this and every other stream
mistakes the monster for itself,
sings its name one final time
then feels the sudden sting of salt.

Christmas Sparrow

The first thing I heard this morning
was a rapid flapping sound, soft, insistent—

wings against glass as it turned out
downstairs when I saw the small bird
rioting in the frame of a high window,
trying to hurl itself through
the enigma of glass into the spacious light.

Then a noise in the throat of the cat
who was hunkered on the rug
told me how the bird had gotten inside,
carried in the cold night
through the flap of a basement door,
and later released from the soft grip of teeth.

On a chair, I trapped its pulsations
in a shirt and got it to the door,
so weightless it seemed
to have vanished into the nest of cloth.

But outside, when I uncupped my hands,
it burst into its element,
dipping over the dormant garden
in a spasm of wingbeats
then disappeared over a row of tall hemlocks.

For the rest of the day,
I could feel its wild thrumming
against my palms as I wondered about
the hours it must have spent
pent in the shadows of that room,
hidden in the spiky branches
of our decorated tree, breathing there
among the metallic angels, ceramic apples, stars of yarn,
its eyes open, like mine as I lie in bed tonight
picturing this rare, lucky sparrow
tucked into a holly bush now,
a light snow tumbling through the windless dark.

Surprise

This—
according to the voice on the radio,
the host of a classical music program no less—
this is the birthday of Vivaldi.

He would be 325 years old today—
quite bent over, I would imagine,
and not able to see much through his watery eyes.

Surely, he would be deaf by now,
the clothes flaking off him,
hair pitiably sparse.

But we would throw a party for him anyway,
a surprise party where everyone
would hide behind the furniture to listen

for the tap of his cane on the pavement
and the sound of that dry, persistent cough.

Poetry

Call it a field where the animals
who were forgotten by the Ark
come to graze under the evening clouds.

Or a cistern where the rain that fell
before history trickles over a concrete lip.

However you see it,
this is no place to set up
the three-legged easel of realism

or make a reader climb
over the many fences of a plot.

Let the portly novelist
with his noisy typewriter
describe the city where Francine was born,

how Albert read the paper on the train,
how curtains were blowing in the bedroom.

Let the playwright with her torn cardigan
and a dog curled on the rug
move the characters

from the wings to the stage
to face the many-eyed darkness of the house.

Poetry is no place for that.
We have enough to do
complaining about the price of tobacco,

passing the dripping ladle,
and singing songs to a bird in a cage.

We are busy doing nothing—
and all we need for that is an afternoon,
a rowboat under a blue sky,

and maybe a man fishing from a stone bridge,
or, better still, nobody on that bridge at all.

FROM *THE TROUBLE WITH POETRY*
(2005)

Monday

The birds are in their trees,
the toast is in the toaster,
and the poets are at their windows.

They are at their windows
in every section of the tangerine of earth—
the Chinese poets looking up at the moon,
the American poets gazing out
at the pink and blue ribbons of sunrise.

The clerks are at their desks,
the miners are down in their mines,
and the poets are looking out their windows
maybe with a cigarette, a cup of tea,
and maybe a flannel shirt or bathrobe is involved.

The proofreaders are playing the ping-pong
game of proofreading,
glancing back and forth from page to page,
the chefs are dicing celery and potatoes,
and the poets are at their windows
because it is their job for which
they are paid nothing every Friday afternoon.

What window it hardly seems to matter
though many have a favorite,

for there is always something to see—
a bird grasping a thin branch,
the headlights of a taxi rounding a corner,
those two boys in wool caps angling across the street.

The fishermen bob in their boats,
the linemen climb their round poles,
the barbers wait by their mirrors and chairs,
and the poets continue to stare
at the cracked birdbath or a limb knocked down by the wind.

By now, it should go without saying
that what the oven is to the baker
and the berry-stained blouse to the drycleaner,
so the window is to the poet.

Just think—
before the invention of the window,
the poets would have had to put on a jacket
and a winter hat to go outside
or remain indoors with only a wall to stare at.

And when I say a wall,
I do not mean a wall with striped wallpaper
and a sketch of a cow in a frame.

I mean a cold wall of field stones,
the wall of the medieval sonnet,
the original woman's heart of stone,
the stone caught in the throat of her poet-lover.

Statues in the Park

I thought of you today
when I stopped before an equestrian statue
in the middle of a public square,

you who had once instructed me
in the code of these noble poses.

A horse rearing up with two legs raised,
you told me, meant the rider had died in battle.

If only one leg was lifted,
the man had elsewhere succumbed to his wounds;

and if four legs were touching the ground,
as they were in this case—
bronze hooves affixed to a stone base—
it meant that the man on the horse,

this one staring intently
over the closed movie theatre across the street,
had died of a cause other than war.

In the shadow of the statue,
I wondered about the others
who had simply walked through life
without a horse, a saddle, or a sword—

pedestrians who could no longer
place one foot in front of the other.

I pictured statues of the sickly
recumbent on their cold stone beds,
the suicides toeing the marble edge,

statues of accident victims covering their eyes,
the murdered covering their wounds,
the drowned silently treading the air.

And there was I,
up on a rosy-gray block of granite
near a cluster of shade trees in the local park,
my name and dates pressed into a plaque,

down on my knees, eyes lifted,
praying to the passing clouds,
forever begging in vain for just one more day.

House

I lie in a bedroom of a house
that was built in 1862, we were told—
the two windows still facing east
into the bright daily reveille of the sun.

The early birds are chirping,
and I think of those who have slept here before,
the family we bought the house from—
the five Critchlows—

and the engineer they told us about
who lived here alone before them,
the one who built onto the back
of the house a large glassy room with wood beams.

I have an old photograph of the house
in black and white, a few small trees,
and a curved dirt driveway,
but I do not know who lived here then.

So I go back to the Civil War
and to the farmer who built the house
and the rough stone walls
that encompass the house and run up into the woods,

he who mounted his thin wife in this room,
while the war raged to the south,
with the strength of a dairyman
or with the tenderness of a dairyman

or with both, alternating back and forth
so as to give his wife much pleasure
and to call down a son to earth
to take over the cows and the farm

when he no longer had the strength
after all the days and nights of toil and prayer—
the sun breaking over the same horizon
into these same windows,

lighting the same bed-space where I lie
having nothing to farm, and no son,
only the dead farmer and his dead wife for company,
feeling hotter and warmer by turns.

The Long Day

In the morning I ate a banana
like a young ape
and worked on a poem called "Nocturne."

In the afternoon I opened the mail
with a short kitchen knife,
and when dusk began to fall

I took off my clothes,
put on "Sweetheart of the Rodeo"
and soaked in a claw-footed bathtub.

I closed my eyes and thought
about the alphabet,
the letters filing out of the halls of kindergarten

to become literature.
If the British call z zed,
I wondered, why not call b bed and d dead.

And why does z, which looks like
the fastest letter, come at the very end?
unless they are all moving east

when we are facing north in our chairs.
It was then that I heard
a clap of thunder and the dog's bark,

and the claw-footed bathtub
took one step forward,
or was it backward

I had to ask
as I turned
to reach for a far-away towel.

In the Evening

The heads of roses begin to droop.
The bee who has been hauling her gold
all day finds a hexagon in which to rest.

In the sky, traces of clouds,
the last few darting birds,
watercolors on the horizon.

The white cat sits facing a wall.
The horse in the field is asleep on its feet.

I light a candle on the wood table.
I take another sip of wine.
I pick up an onion and a knife.

And the past and the future?
Nothing but an only child with two different masks.

Flock

It has been calculated that each copy of
the Gutenburg Bible . . . required the
skins of 300 sheep.

—from an article on printing

I can see them squeezed into the holding pen
behind the stone building
where the printing press is housed,

all of them squirming around
to find a little room
and looking so much alike

it would be nearly impossible
to count them,
and there is no telling

which one will carry the news
that the Lord is a shepherd,
one of the few things they already know.

Building with Its Face Blown Off

How suddenly the private
is revealed in a bombed out city,
how the blue and white striped wallpaper

of a second story bedroom is now
exposed to the lightly falling snow
as if the room had answered the explosion

wearing only its striped pajamas.
Some neighbors and soldiers
poke around in the rubble below

and stare up at the hanging staircase,
the portrait of a grandfather,
a door dangling from a single hinge.

And the bathroom looks almost embarrassed
by its uncovered ochre walls,
the twisted mess of its plumbing,

the sink sinking to its knees,
the ripped shower curtain,
the torn goldfish trailing bubbles.

It's like a dollhouse view
as if a child on its knees could reach in
and pick up the bureau, straighten a picture.

Or it might be a room on a stage
in a play with no characters,
no dialogue or audience,

no beginning, middle and end—
just the broken furniture in the street,
a shoe among the cinder blocks,

a light snow still falling
on a distant steeple, and people
crossing a bridge that still stands.

And beyond that—crows in a tree,
the statue of a leader on a horse,
and clouds that could be smoke,

and even farther on, in another country
on a blanket under a shade tree,
a man pouring wine into two glasses

and a woman sliding out
the wooden pegs of a wicker hamper
filled with bread, cheese, and several kinds of olives.

The Lanyard

The other day as I was ricocheting slowly
off the pale blue walls of this room,
bouncing from typewriter to piano,
from bookshelf to an envelope lying on the floor,
I found myself in the L section of the dictionary
where my eyes fell upon the word *lanyard*.

No cookie nibbled by a French novelist
could send one more suddenly into the past—
a past where I sat at a workbench at a camp
by a deep Adirondack lake
learning how to braid thin plastic strips
into a lanyard, a gift for my mother.

I had never seen anyone use a lanyard
or wear one, if that's what you did with them,
but that did not keep me from crossing
strand over strand again and again
until I had made a boxy
red and white lanyard for my mother.

She gave me life and milk from her breasts,
and I gave her a lanyard.
She nursed me in many a sick room,
lifted teaspoons of medicine to my lips,

set cold face-cloths on my forehead,
and then led me out into the airy light

and taught me to walk and swim,
and I, in turn, presented her with a lanyard.
Here are thousands of meals, she said,
and here is clothing and a good education.
And here is your lanyard, I replied,
which I made with a little help from a counselor.

Here is a breathing body and a beating heart,
strong legs, bones and teeth,
and two clear eyes to read the world, she whispered,
and here, I said, is the lanyard I made at camp.
And here, I wish to say to her now,
is a smaller gift—not the archaic truth

that you can never repay your mother,
but the rueful admission that when she took
the two-tone lanyard from my hands,
I was as sure as a boy could be
that this useless, worthless thing I wove
out of boredom would be enough to make us even.

Boy Shooting at a Statue

It was late afternoon,
the beginning of winter, a light snow,
and I was the only one in the small park

to witness the lone boy running
in circles around the base of a bronze statue.
I could not read the carved name

of the statesman who loomed above,
one hand on his cold hip,
but as the boy ran, head down,

he would point a finger at the statue
and pull an imaginary trigger
imitating the sounds of rapid gunfire.

Evening thickened, the mercury sank,
but the boy kept running in the circle
of his footprints in the snow

shooting blindly into the air.
History will never find a way to end,
I thought, as I left the park by the north gate

and walked slowly home
returning to the station of my desk
where the sheets of paper I wrote on

were like pieces of glass
through which I could see
hundreds of dark birds circling in the sky below.

Genius

was what they called you in high school
if you tripped on a shoelace in the hall
and all your books went flying.

Or if you walked into an open locker door,
you would be known as Einstein,
who imagined riding a streetcar into infinity.

Later, genius became someone
who could take a sliver of chalk and squire pi
a hundred places out beyond the decimal point,

or a man painting on his back on a scaffold,
or drawing a waterwheel in a margin,
or spinning out a little night music.

But earlier this week on a wooded path,
I thought the swans afloat on the reservoir
were the true geniuses,

the ones who had figured out how to fly,
how to be both beautiful and brutal,
and how to mate for life.

Twenty-four geniuses in all,
for I numbered them as Yeats had done,
deployed upon the calm, crystalline surface—

forty-eight if we count their white reflections,
or an even fifty if you want to throw in me
and the dog running up ahead,

who were at least smart enough to be out
that morning—she sniffing the ground,
me with my head up in the bright morning air.

The Order of the Day

A morning after a week of rain
and the sun shot down through the branches
into the tall, bare windows.

The brindled cat rolled over on his back,
and I could hear you in the kitchen
grinding coffee beans into a powder.

Everything seemed especially vivid
because I knew we were all going to die,
first the cat, then you, then me,

then somewhat later the liquefied sun
was the order I was envisioning.
But then again, you never really know.

The cat had a fiercely healthy look,
his coat so bristling and electric
I wondered what you had been feeding him

and what you had been feeding me
as I turned a corner
and beheld you out there on the sunny deck

lost in exercise, running in place,
knees lifted high, skin glistening—
and that toothy, immortal-looking smile of yours.

The Centrifuge

It is difficult to describe what we felt
after we paid the admission,
entered the aluminum dome,

and stood there with our mouths open
before the machine itself,
what we had only read about in the papers.

Huge and glistening it was
but bolted down and giving nothing away.

What did it mean?
we all openly wondered,
and did another machine exist somewhere else—
an even mightier one—
that was designed to be its exact opposite?

These were not new questions,
but we asked them earnestly and repeatedly.

Later, when we were home again—
a family of six having tea—
we raised these questions once more,
knowing that this made us part
of a great historical discussion

that included science
as well as literature and the weather

not to mention the lodger downstairs,
who, someone said,
had been seen earlier leaving the house
with a suitcase and a tightly furled umbrella.

The Revenant

I am the dog you put to sleep,
as you like to call the needle of oblivion,
come back to tell you this simple thing:
I never liked you—not one bit.

When I licked your face,
I thought of biting off your nose.
When I watched you toweling yourself dry,
I wanted to leap and unman you with a snap.

I resented the way you moved,
your lack of animal grace,
the way you would sit in a chair to eat,
a napkin on your lap, knife in your hand.

I would have run away,
but I was too weak, a trick you taught me
while I was learning to sit and heel,
and—greatest of insults—shake hands without a hand.

I admit the sight of the leash
would excite me
but only because it meant I was about
to smell things you had never touched.

You do not want to believe this,
but I have no reason to lie.
I hated the car, the rubber toys,
disliked your friends and, worse, your relatives.

The jingling of my tags drove me mad.
You always scratched me in the wrong place.
All I ever wanted from you
was food and fresh water in my metal bowls.

While you slept, I watched you breathe
as the moon rose in the sky.
It took all of my strength
not to raise my head and howl.

Now I am free of the collar,
the yellow raincoat, monogrammed sweater,
the absurdity of your lawn,
and that is all you need to know about this place

except what you already supposed
and are glad it did not happen sooner—
that everyone here can read and write,
the dogs in poetry, the cats and all the others in prose.

Carry

I want to carry you
and for you to carry me
the way voices are said to carry over water.

Just this morning on the shore,
I could hear two people talking quietly
in a row boat on the far side of the lake.

They were talking about fishing,
then one changed the subject,
and, I swear, they began talking about you.

Fool Me Good

I am under the covers
waiting for the heat to come up
with a gurgle and hiss
and the banging of the water hammer
that will frighten the cold out of the room.

And I am listening to a blues singer
named Precious Bryant
singing a song called "Fool Me Good."

If you don't love me, baby, she sings,
would you please try to fool me good?

I am also stroking the dog's head
and writing down these words,
which means that I am calmly flying
in the face of the Buddhist advice
to do only one thing at a time.

Just pour the tea,
just look into the eye of the flower,
just sing the song—
one thing at a time
and you will achieve serenity,
which is what I would love to do
as the fan-blades of the morning begin to turn.

If you don't love me, baby,
she sings,
as a day-moon fades in the window,
and the hands circle the clock,
would you please try to fool me good?

Yes, Precious, I reply,
I will fool you as good as I can,
but first I have to learn to listen to you
with my whole heart,
and not until you have finished

will I put on my slippers,
squeeze out some toothpaste,
and make a big foamy face in the mirror,

freshly dedicated to doing one thing at a time—
one note at a time for you, darling,
one tooth at a time for me.

The Trouble with Poetry

The trouble with poetry, I realized
as I walked along a beach one night—
cold Florida sand under my bare feet,
a show of stars in the sky—

the trouble with poetry is
that it encourages the writing of more poetry,
more guppies crowding the fish tank,
more baby rabbits
hopping out of their mothers into the dewy grass.

And how will it ever end?
unless the day finally arrives
when we have compared everything in the world
to everything else in the world,

and there is nothing left to do
but quietly close our notebooks
and sit with our hands folded on our desks.

Poetry fills me with joy
and I rise like a feather in the wind.
Poetry fills me with sorrow
and I sink like a chain flung from a bridge.

But mostly poetry fills me
with the urge to write poetry,
to sit in the dark and wait for a little flame
to appear at the tip of my pencil.

And along with that, the longing to steal,
to break into the poems of others
with a flashlight and a ski mask.

And what an unmerry band of thieves we are,
cut-purses, common shoplifters,
I thought to myself
as a cold wave swirled around my feet
and the lighthouse moved its megaphone over the sea,
which is an image I stole directly
from Lawrence Ferlinghetti—
to be perfectly honest for a moment—

the bicycling poet of San Francisco
whose little amusement park of a book
I carried in a side pocket of my uniform
up and down the treacherous halls of high school.

FROM *BALLISTICS*
(2008)

Brightly Colored Boats Upturned on the Banks of the Charles

What is there to say about them
that has not been said in the title?
I saw them near dawn from a glassy room
on the other side of that river,
which flowed from some hidden spring
to the sea; but that is getting away from
the brightly colored boats upturned
on the banks of the Charles,
the sleek racing sculls of a college crew team.

They were beautiful in the clear early light—
red, yellow, blue and green—
is all I wanted to say about them,
although for the rest of the day
I pictured a lighter version of myself
calling time through a little megaphone,
first to the months of the year,
then to the twelve apostles, all grimacing
as they leaned and pulled on the long wooden oars.

Searching

I recall someone once admitting
that all he remembered of *Anna Karenina*
was something about a picnic basket,

and now, after consuming a book
devoted to the subject of Barcelona—
its people, its history, its complex architecture—

all I remember is the mention
of an albino gorilla, the inhabitant of a park
where the Citadel of the Bourbons once stood.

The sheer paleness of her looms over
all the notable names and dates
as the evening strollers stop before her

and point to show their children.
These locals called her Snowflake,
and here she has been mentioned again in print

in the hope of keeping her pallid flame alive
and helping her, despite her name, to endure
in this poem where she has found another cage.

Oh, Snowflake,
I had no interest in the capital of Catalonia—
its people, its history, its complex architecture—

no, you were the reason
I kept my light on late into the night
turning all those pages, searching for you everywhere.

High

On that clear October morning,
I was only behind a double espresso
and a single hit of anti-depressant,

yet there, on the shore of the reservoir
with its flipped-over row boats,
I felt like I was walking with Jane Austen

to borrow the jargon of the streets.
Yes, I was wearing the crown,
as the drug addicts like to say,

knitting a bonnet for Charlie,
entertaining the troops,
sitting in the study with H.G. Wells—

so many ways to express that mood
of royal goodwill
when the gift of sight is cause enough for jubilation.

And later in the afternoon
when I finally came down,
a lexicon was waiting for me there, too.

In my upholstered chair by a window
with dusk pouring into the room,
I appeared to be doing nothing,

but inside I was busy riding the marble,
as the lurkers like to put it—
talking to Marco Polo,

juggling turtles,
going through the spin cycle,
or—my favorite, if I had to have one—out of milk.

The Four-Moon Planet

I have envied the four-moon planet.

—The Notebooks of Robert Frost

Maybe he was thinking of the song
"What a Little Moonlight Can Do"
and became curious about
what a lot of moonlight might be capable of.

But wouldn't this be too much of a good thing?
and what if you couldn't tell them apart
and they always rose together
like pale quadruplets entering a living room.

Yes, there would be enough light
to read a book or write a letter at midnight,
and if you drank enough tequila
you might see eight of them roving brightly above.

But think of the two lovers on a beach,
his arm around her bare shoulder,
thrilled at how close they were feeling tonight
while he gazed at one moon and she another.

No Things

This love for everyday things,
part natural from the wide eye of infancy,
part a literary calculation,

this attention to the morning flower
and later to a fly strolling
along the rim of a wineglass—

are we just avoiding our one true destiny
when we do that, averting our glance
from Philip Larkin who waits for us in an undertaker's coat?

The leafless branches against the sky
will not save anyone from the void ahead,
nor will the sugar bowl or the sugar spoon on the table.

So why bother with the checkered lighthouse?
Why waste time on the sparrow,
or the wildflowers along the roadside

when we all should be alone in our rooms
throwing ourselves at the wall of life
and the opposite wall of death,

the door locked behind us
as we hurl rocks at the question of meaning
and the enigma of our origins?

What good is the firefly,
the droplet running along the green leaf,
or even the bar of soap sliding around the bathtub

when we are really meant to be
banging away on the mystery
as hard as we can and to hell with the neighbors?

banging away on nothingness itself,
some with their foreheads,
others with the maul of sense, the raised jawbone of poetry.

The First Night

> The worst thing about death must be
> the first night.
>
> —Jose Ramón Jiménez

Before I opened you, Jiménez,
it never occurred to me that day and night
would continue to circle each other in the ring of death,

but now you have me wondering
if there will also be a sun and a moon
and will the dead gather to watch them rise and set

then repair, each soul alone,
to some ghastly equivalent of a bed.
Or will the first night be the only night,

a long darkness for which we have no other name?
How feeble our vocabulary in the face of death,
How impossible to write it down.

This is where language will stop,
the horse we have ridden all our lives
rearing up at the edge of a dizzying cliff.

The word that was in the beginning
and the word that was made flesh—
those and all the other words will cease.

Even now, reading you on this trellised porch,
how can I describe a sun that will shine after death?
But it is enough to frighten me

into paying more attention to the world's day-moon,
to sunlight bright on water
or fragmented in a grove of trees,

and to look more closely here at these small leaves,
these sentinel thorns,
whose employment it is to guard the rose.

January in Paris

> Poems are never completed—they are
> only abandoned.
>
> —Paul Valéry

That winter I had nothing to do
but tend the kettle in my shuttered room
on the top floor of a pensione near a cemetery,

but I would sometimes descend the stairs,
unlock my bicycle, and pedal along the cold city streets
often turning from a wide boulevard
down a narrow side street
bearing the name of an obscure patriot.

I followed a few private rules,
never crossing a bridge without stopping
mid-point to lean my bike on the railing
and observe the flow of the river below
as I tried to better understand the French.

In my pale coat and my Basque cap
I pedaled past the windows of a patisserie
or sat up tall in the seat, arms folded,
and clicked downhill filling my nose with winter air.

I would see beggars and street cleaners
in their bright uniforms, and sometimes
I would see the poems of Valéry,
the ones he never finished but abandoned,
wandering the streets of the city half-clothed.

Most of them needed only a final line
or two, a little verbal flourish at the end,
but whenever I approached,
they would retreat from their ashcan fires
into the shadows—thin specters of incompletion,

forsaken for so many long decades
how could they ever trust another man with a pen?

I came across the one I wanted to tell you about
sitting with a glass of rosé at a café table—
beautiful, emaciated, unfinished,
cruelly abandoned with a flick of panache

by Monsieur Paul Valéry himself,
big fish in the school of Symbolism
and for a time, president of the Committee of Arts and Letters
of the League of Nations if you please.

Never mind how I got her out of the café,
past the concierge and up the flights of stairs—
remember that Paris is the capital of public kissing.

And never mind the holding and the pressing.
It is enough to know that I moved my pen
in such a way as to bring her to completion,

a simple, final stanza, which ended,
as this poem will, with the image
of a gorgeous orphan lying on a rumpled bed,
her large eyes closed,
a painting of cows in a valley over her head,

and off to the side, me in a window seat
blowing smoke from a cigarette at dawn.

Ballistics

When I came across the high-speed photograph
of a bullet that had just pierced a book—
the pages exploding with the velocity—

I forgot all about the marvels of photography
and began to wonder which book
the photographer had selected for the shot.

Many novels sprang to mind
including those of Raymond Chandler
where an extra bullet would hardly be noticed.

Non-fiction offered too many choices—
a history of Scottish lighthouses,
a biography of Joan of Arc and so forth.

Or it could be an anthology of medieval literature,
the bullet having just beheaded Sir Gawain
and scattered the band of assorted pilgrims.

But later, as I was drifting off to sleep,
I realized that the executed book
was a recent collection of poems written

by someone of whom I was not fond
and that the bullet must have passed through
his writing with little resistance

at twenty-eight-hundred feet per second,
through the poems about his sorry childhood
and the ones about the dreary state of the world,

and then through the author's photograph,
through the beard, the round glasses,
and that special poet's hat he loves to wear.

Pornography

In this sentimental painting of rustic life,
a rosy-cheeked fellow
in a broad hat and ballooning green pants

is twirling a peasant girl in a red frock
while a boy is playing a squeeze-box
near a turned-over barrel

upon which rest a knife, a jug, and small drinking glass.
Two men in rough jackets
are playing cards at a wooden table.

And in the background a woman in a bonnet
stands behind a half-open Dutch door
talking to a merchant or a beggar who is leaning on a cane.

This is all I need to inject me with desire,
to fill me with the urge to lie down with you,
or someone very much like you

on a cool marble floor or any fairly flat surface
as clouds go flying by
and the rustle of tall leafy trees

mixes with the notes of birdsong—
so clearly does the work speak to me of vanishing time,
obsolete musical instruments,

passing fancies, and the corpse
of the largely forgotten painter moldering
somewhere beneath the surface of present-day France.

Greek and Roman Statuary

The tip of the nose seemed the first to be lost,
then the arms and legs,
and later the stone penis if such a thing were featured.

And often an entire head followed the nose
as it might have done when bread
was baking in the side streets of ancient Rome.

No hope for the flute once attached
to the lips of that satyr with the puffed-out cheeks,
nor for the staff the shepherd boy once leaned on,

the sword no longer gripped by the warrior,
the poor lost ears of the sleeping boy,
and whatever it was Aphrodite once held in her severed hand.

But the torso is another story—
middle man, the last to go, bluntly surviving,
propped up on a pedestal with a length of pipe,

and the mighty stone ass endures,
so smooth and fundamental, no one
hesitates to leave the group and walk behind to stare.

And that is the way it goes here
in the diffused light from the translucent roof,
one missing extremity after another—

digits that got too close to the slicer of time,
hands snapped off by the clock,
whole limbs caught in the mortal thresher.

But outside on the city streets,
it is raining, and the pavement shines
with the crisscross traffic of living bodies—

hundreds of noses still intact,
arms swinging and hands grasping,
the skin still warm and foreheads glistening.

It's anyone's guess when the day will come
when there is nothing left of us
but the bare, solid plinth we once stood upon

now exposed to the open air,
just the wind in the trees and the shadows
of clouds sweeping over its hard marble surface.

Scenes of Hell

We did not have the benefit of a guide,
no crone to lead us off the common path,
no ancient to point the way with a staff,

but there were badlands to cross,
rivers of fire and blackened peaks,
and eventually we could look down and see

the jeweler running around a gold ring,
the boss trapped in an hour glass,
the baker buried up to his eyes in flour,

the banker plummeting on a coin,
the teacher disappearing into a blackboard,
and the grocer silent under a pyramid of vegetables.

We saw the pilot nose-diving
and the whore impaled on a bedpost,
the pharmacist wandering in a stupor

and the child with toy wheels for legs.
You pointed to the soldier
who was dancing with his empty uniform

and I remarked on the blind tourist.
But what truly caught our attention
was the scene in the long mirror of ice:

you lighting the wick on your head,
me blowing on the final spark,
and our children trying to crawl away from their eggshells.

Hippos on Holiday

is not really the title of a movie
but if it were I would be sure to see it.
I love their short legs and big heads,
the whole hippo look.
Hundreds of them would frolic
in the mud of a wide, slow-moving river,
and I would eat my popcorn
in the dark of a neighborhood theatre.
When they opened their enormous mouths
lined with big stubby teeth
I would drink my enormous Coke.

I would be both in my seat
and in the water playing with the hippos,
which is the way it is
with a truly great movie.
Only a mean-spirited reviewer
would ask on holiday from what?

Lost

There was no art in losing that coin
you gave me for luck, the one with the profile
of an emperor on one side and a palm on the other.

It rode for days in a pocket
of my black pants, the paint-speckled ones,
past storefronts, gas stations and playgrounds,

and then it was gone, as lost as the lost
theorems of Pythagoras, or the *Medea* by Ovid,
which also slipped through the bars of time,

and as ungraspable as the sin that landed him—
forever out of favor with Augustus—
on a cold rock on the coast of the Black Sea,

where eventually he died, but not before
writing a poem about the fish of those waters,
into which, as we know, he was never transformed,

nor into a flower, a tree, or a stream,
nor into a star like Julius Caesar,
not even into a small bird that could wing it back to Rome.

Tension

Never use the word *suddenly* just to
create tension.

— *Writing Fiction*

Suddenly, you were planting some yellow petunias
outside in the garden,
and suddenly I was in the study
looking up the word *oligarchy* for the thirty-seventh time.

When suddenly, without warning,
you planted the last petunia in the flat,
and I suddenly closed the dictionary
now that I was reminded of that vile form of governance.

A moment later, we found ourselves
standing suddenly in the kitchen
where you suddenly opened a can of cat food
and I just as suddenly watched you doing that.

I observed a window of leafy activity
and beyond that, a bird perched on the edge
of the stone birdbath
when suddenly you announced you were leaving

to pick up a few things at the market
and I stunned you by impulsively
pointing out that we were getting low on butter
and another case of wine would not be a bad idea.

Who could tell what the next moment would hold?
another drip from the faucet?
another little spasm of the second hand?
Would the painting of a bowl of pears continue

to hang on the wall from that nail?
Would the heavy anthologies remain on their shelves?
Would the stove hold its position?
Suddenly, it was anyone's guess.

The sun rose ever higher in the sky.
The state capitals remained motionless on the wall map
when suddenly I found myself lying on a couch
where I closed my eyes and without any warning

began to picture the Andes, of all places,
and a path that led over the mountains to another country
with strange customs and eye-catching hats
each one suddenly fringed with colorful little tassels.

The Golden Years

All I do these drawn-out days
is sit in my kitchen at Pheasant Ridge
where there are no pheasant to be seen
and last time I looked, no ridge.

I could drive over to Quail Falls
and spend the day there playing bridge,
but the lack of a falls and the absence of quail
would only remind me of Pheasant Ridge.

I know a widow at Fox Run
and another with a condo at Smokey Ledge.
One of them smokes, and neither can run,
so I'll stick to the pledge I made to Midge.

Who frightened the fox and bulldozed the ledge?
I ask in my kitchen at Pheasant Ridge.

(detail)

It was getting late in the year,
the sky had been low and overcast for days,
and I was drinking tea in a glassy room
with a woman without children,
a gate through which no one had entered the world.

She was turning the pages of an expensive book
on a coffee table, even though we were drinking tea,
a book of colorful paintings—
a landscape, a portrait, a still life,
a field, a face, a pear and a knife, all turning on the table.

Men had entered there but no girl or boy
had come out, I was thinking oddly
as she stopped at a page of clouds
aloft in a pale sky, tinged with red and gold.
This one is my favorite, she said,

even though it was only a detail, a corner
of a larger painting which she had never seen.
Nor did she want to see the countryside below
or the portrayal of some myth
in order for the billowing clouds to seem complete.

This was enough, this fraction of the whole,
just as the leafy scene in the windows was enough
now that the light was growing dim,
as was she enough, perfectly by herself
somewhere in the enormous mural of the world.

Adage

When it's late at night and branches
are banging against the windows,
you might think that love is just a matter

of leaping out of the frying pan of yourself
into the fire of someone else,
but it's a little more complicated than that.

It's more like trading the two birds
who might be hiding in that bush
for the one you are not holding in your hand.

A wise man once said that love
was like forcing a horse to drink
but then everyone stopped thinking of him as wise.

Let us be clear about something.
Love is not as simple as getting up
on the wrong side of the bed wearing the emperor's clothes.

No, it's more like the way the pen
feels after it has defeated the sword.
It's a little like the penny saved or the nine dropped stitches.

You look at me through the halo of the last candle
and tell me love is an ill wind
that has no turning, a road that blows no good,

but I am here to remind you,
as our shadows tremble on the walls,
that love is the early bird who is better late than never.

The Flight of the Statues

The ancient Greeks . . . used to chain
their statues to prevent them from fleeing.

—Michael Kimmelman

It might have been the darkening sky
that sent them running in all directions
that afternoon as the air turned a pale yellow,

but were they not used to standing out
in the squares of our city
in every kind of imaginable weather?

Maybe they were frightened by a headline
on a newspaper that was blowing by
or was it the children in their martial arts uniforms?

Did they finally learn about the humans
they stood for as they pointed a sword at a cloud?
Did they know something we did not?

Whatever the cause, no one will forget
the sight of all the white marble figures
leaping from their pedestals and rushing away.

In the parks, the guitarists fell silent.
The vendor froze under his umbrella.
A dog tried to hide in his owner's shadow.

Even the chess players under the trees
looked up from their boards
long enough to see the bronze generals

dismount and run off, leaving their horses
to peer down at the circling pigeons
who were stealing a few more crumbs from the poor.

Baby Listening

According to the guest information directory,
baby listening is a service offered by this seaside hotel.

Baby-listening—not a baby who happens to be listening,
as I thought when I first checked in.

Leave the receiver off the hook,
the directory advises,
and your infant can be monitored by the staff,

though the staff, the entry continues,
cannot be held responsible for the well-being
of the baby in question.

Fair enough: someone to listen to the baby.

But the phrase did suggest a baby who is listening,
lying there in the room next to mine
listening to my pen scratching against the page,

or a more advanced baby who has crawled
down the hallway of the hotel
and is pressing its tiny, curious ear against my door.

Lucky for some of us,
poetry is a place where both are true at once,
where meaning only one thing at a time spells malfunction.

Poetry wants to have the baby who is listening at my door
as well as the baby who is being listened to,
quietly breathing into the nearby telephone.

And it also wants the baby
who is making sounds of distress
into the curved receiver lying in the crib

while the girl at reception has just stepped out
to have a smoke with her boyfriend
in the dark by the great wash and sway of the North Sea.

Poetry wants that baby, too,
even a little more than it wants the others.

Bathtub Families

is not just a phrase I made up
though it would have given me pleasure
to have written those words in a notebook
then looked up at the sky wondering what they meant.

No, I saw Bathtub Families in a pharmacy
on the label of a clear plastic package
containing one cow and four calves,
a little family of animals meant to float in your tub.

I hesitated to buy it because I knew
I would then want the entire series of Bathtub Families,
which would leave no room in the tub
for the turtles, the pigs, the seals, the giraffes, and me.

It's enough just to have the words,
which alone make me even more grateful
that I was born in America
and English is my mother tongue.

I was lucky, too, that I waited
for the pharmacist to fill my prescription,
otherwise I might not have wandered
down the aisle with the Bathtub Families.

I think what I am really saying is that language
is better than reality, so it doesn't have
to be bath time for you to enjoy
all the Bathtub Families as they float in the air around your head.

The Fish

As soon as the elderly waiter
placed before me the fish I had ordered,
it began to stare up at me
with its one flat, iridescent eye.

I feel sorry for you, it seemed to say,
eating alone in this awful restaurant
bathed in such unkindly light
and surrounded by these dreadful murals of Sicily.

And I feel sorry for you, too—
yanked from the sea and now lying dead
next to some boiled potatoes in Pittsburgh—
I said back to the fish as I raised my fork.

And thus my dinner in an unfamiliar city
with its rivers and lighted bridges
was graced not only with chilled wine
and lemon slices but with compassion and sorrow

even after the waiter had removed my plate
with the head of the fish still staring
and the barrel vault of its delicate bones
terribly exposed, save for a shroud of parsley.

A Dog on His Master

As young as I look,
I am growing older faster than he,
seven to one
is the ratio they tend to say.

Whatever the number,
I will pass him one day
and take the lead
the way I do on our walks in the woods.

And if this ever manages
to cross his mind,
it would be the sweetest
shadow I have ever cast on snow or grass.

The Great American Poem

If this were a novel,
it would begin with a character,
a man alone on a southbound train
or a young girl on a swing by a farmhouse.

And as the pages turned, you would be told
that it was morning or the dead of night,
and I, the narrator, would describe
for you the miscellaneous clouds over the farmhouse

and what the man was wearing on the train
right down to his red tartan scarf,
and the hat he tossed onto the rack above his head,
as well as the cows sliding past his window.

Eventually—one can only read so fast—
you would learn either that the train was bearing
the man back to the place of his birth
or that he was headed into the vast unknown,

and you might just tolerate all of this
as you waited patiently for shots to ring out
in a ravine where the man was hiding
or for a tall, raven-haired woman to appear in a doorway.

But this is a poem,
and the only characters here are you and I,
alone in an imaginary room
which will disappear after a few more lines,

leaving us no time to point guns at one another
or toss all our clothes into a roaring fireplace.
I ask you: who needs the man on the train
and who cares what his black valise contains?

We have something better than all this turbulence
lurching toward some ruinous conclusion.
I mean the sound that we will hear
as soon as I stop writing and put down this pen.

I once heard someone compare it
to the sound of crickets in a field of wheat
or, more faintly, just the wind
over that field stirring things that we will never see.

Divorce

Once, two spoons in bed,
now tined forks

across a granite table
and the knives they have hired.

This Little Piggy Went to Market

is the usual thing to say when you begin
pulling on the toes of a small child,
and I have never had a problem with that.
I could easily picture the piggy with his basket
and his trotters kicking up the dust on an imaginary road.

What always stopped me in my tracks was
the middle toe—this little piggy ate roast beef.
I mean I enjoy a roast beef sandwich
with lettuce and tomato and a dollop of horseradish,
but I cannot see a pig ordering that in a delicatessen.

I am probably being too literal-minded here—
I am even wondering why it's called "horseradish."
I should just go along with the beautiful nonsense
of the nursery, float downstream on its waters.
After all, Little Jack Horner speaks to me deeply.

I don't want to be the one to ruin the children's party
by asking unnecessary questions about Puss in Boots
or, again, the implications of a pig eating beef.
By the way, I am completely down with going
"Wee wee wee" all the way home,
having done that many times and knowing exactly how it feels.

Old Man Eating Alone in a Chinese Restaurant

I am glad I resisted the temptation,
if it was a temptation when I was young,
to write a poem about an old man
eating alone at a corner table in a Chinese restaurant.

I would have gotten it all wrong
thinking: the poor bastard, not a friend in the world
and with only a book for a companion.
He'll probably pay the bill out of a change purse.

So glad I waited all these decades
to record how hot and sour the hot and sour soup is
here at Chang's this afternoon
and how cold the Chinese beer in a frosted glass.

And my book—José Saramago's *Blindness*
as it turns out—is so absorbing that I look up
from its escalating horrors only
when I am stunned by one of its arresting sentences.

And I should mention the light
which falls through the big windows this time of day
italicizing everything it touches—
the plates and tea pots, the immaculate tablecloths,

as well as the soft brown hair of the waitress
in the white blouse and short black skirt,
the one who is smiling now as she bears a cup of rice
and shredded beef with garlic to my favorite table in the corner.

Oh, My God!

Not only in church
and nightly by their bedsides
do young girls pray these days.

Wherever they go,
prayer is woven into their talk
like a bright thread of awe.

Even at the pedestrian mall
outbursts of praise
spring unbidden from their glossy lips.

The Future

When I finally arrive there—
and it will take many days and nights—
I would like to believe others will be waiting
and might even want to know how it was.

So I will reminisce about a particular sky
or a woman in a white bathrobe
or the time I visited a narrow strait
where a famous naval battle had taken place.

Then I will spread out on a table
a large map of my world
and explain to the people of the future
in their pale garments what it was like—

how mountains rose between the valleys
and this was called geography,
how boats loaded with cargo plied the rivers
and this was known as commerce,

how the people from this pink area
crossed over into this light-green area
and set fires and killed whoever they found
and this was called history—

and they will listen, mild-eyed and silent,
as more of them arrive to join the circle,
like ripples moving toward,
not away from, a stone tossed into a pond.

Envoy

Go, little book,
out of this house and into the world,

carriage made of paper rolling toward town
bearing a single passenger
beyond the reach of this jittery pen
and far from the desk and the nosy gooseneck lamp.

It is time to decamp,
put on a jacket and venture outside,
time to be regarded by other eyes,
bound to be held in foreign hands.

So off you go, infants of the brain,
with a wave and some bits of fatherly advice:

stay out as late as you like,
don't bother to call or write,
and talk to as many strangers as you can.

FROM *HOROSCOPES FOR THE DEAD*
(2011)

Grave

What do you think of my new glasses
I asked as I stood under a shade tree
before the joined grave of my parents,

and what followed was a long silence
that descended on the rows of the dead
and on the fields and the woods beyond,

one of the one hundred kinds of silence
according to the Chinese belief,
each one distinct from the others,

and the differences being so faint
that only a few special monks
were able to tell them all apart.

They make you look very scholarly,
I heard my mother say
once I lay down on the ground

and pressed an ear into the soft grass.
Then I rolled over and pressed
my other ear to the ground,

the ear my father likes to speak into,
but he would say nothing,
and I could not find a silence

among the 100 Chinese silences
that would fit the one that he created
even though I was the one

who had just made up the business
of the 100 Chinese silences—
the Silence of the Night Boat,

and the Silence of the Lotus,
cousin to the Silence of the Temple Bell
only deeper and softer, like petals, at its farthest edges.

Palermo

It was foolish of us to leave our room.
The empty plaza was shimmering.
The clock looked ready to melt.

The heat was a mallet striking a ball
and sending it bouncing into the nettles of summer.
Even the bees had knocked off for the day.

The only thing moving besides us
(and we had since stopped under an awning)
was a squirrel who was darting this way and that

as if he were having second thoughts
about crossing the street,
his head and tail twitching with indecision.

You were looking in a shop window
but I was watching the squirrel
who now rose up on his hind legs,

and after pausing to look in all directions,
began to sing in a beautiful voice
a melancholy aria about life and death,

his forepaws clutched against his chest,
his face full of longing and hope,
as the sun beat down

on the roofs and awnings of the city,
and the earth continued to turn
and hold in position the moon

which would appear later that night
as we sat in a café
and I stood up on the table

with the encouragement of the owner
and sang for you and the others
the song the squirrel had taught me how to sing.

Memento Mori

It doesn't take much to remind me
what a mayfly I am,
what a soap bubble floating over the children's party.

Standing under the bones of a dinosaur
in a museum does the trick every time
or confronting in a vitrine a rock from the moon.

Even the Church of St. Anne will do,
a structure I just noticed in a magazine—
built in 1722 of sandstone and limestone in the city of Cork.

And the realization that no one
who ever breasted the waters of time
has figured out a way to avoid dying

always pulls me up by the reins and settles me down
by a roadside, grateful for the sweet weeds
and the mouthfuls of colorful wildflowers.

So many reminders of my mortality
here, there, and elsewhere, visible at every hour,
pretty much everything I can think of except you,

sign over the door of this bar in Cocoa Beach
proclaiming that it was established—
though *established* does not sound right—in 1996.

The Guest

I know the reason you placed nine white tulips
in a glass vase with water
here in this room a few days ago

was not to mark the passage of time
as a fish would have if nailed by the tail
to the wall above the bed of a guest.

But early this morning I did notice
their lowered heads
in the gray light,

two of them even touching the glass
table top near the window,
the blossoms falling open

as they lost their grip on themselves,
and my suitcase only half unpacked by the door.

Gold

I don't want to make too much of this,
but because the bedroom faces east
across a lake here in Florida,

when the sun begins to rise
and reflects off the water,
the whole room is suffused with the kind

of golden light that might travel
at dawn on the summer solstice
the length of a passageway in a megalithic tomb.

Again, I don't want to exaggerate,
but it reminds me of a brand of light
that could illuminate the walls
of a hidden chamber full of treasure,
pearls and gold coins overflowing the silver platters.

I feel like comparing it to the fire
that Aphrodite lit in the human eye
so as to make it possible for us to perceive
the other three elements,

but the last thing I want to do
is risk losing your confidence
by appearing to lay it on too thick.

Let's just say that the morning light here
would bring to any person's mind
the rings of light that Dante

deploys in the final cantos of the *Paradiso*
to convey the presence of God,
while bringing the *Divine Comedy*
to a stunning climax and leave it at that.

Genesis

It was late, of course,
just the two of us still at the table
working on a second bottle of wine

when you speculated that maybe Eve came first
and Adam began as a rib
that leaped out of her side one paradisal afternoon.

Could be, I remember saying,
because much was possible back then,
and I mentioned the talking snake
and the giraffes sticking their necks out of the ark,
their noses up in the pouring Old Testament rain.

I like a man with a flexible mind, you said then,
lifting your candle-lit glass to me
and I raised mine to you and began to wonder

what life would be like as one of your ribs—
to be with you all the time,
riding under your blouse and skin,
caged under the soft weight of your breasts,

your favorite rib, I am assuming,
if you ever bothered to stop and count them

which is just what I did later that night
after you had fallen asleep
and we were fitted tightly back to front,
your long legs against the length of mine,
my fingers doing the crazy numbering that comes of love.

Horoscopes for the Dead

Every morning since you disappeared for good,
I read about you in the newspaper
along with the box scores, the weather, and all the bad news.

Some days I am reminded that today
will not be a wildly romantic time for you,
nor will you be challenged by educational goals,
nor will you need to be circumspect at the workplace.

Another day, I learn that you should not miss
an opportunity to travel and make new friends
though you never cared much about either.

I can't imagine you ever facing a new problem
with a positive attitude, but you will definitely not
be doing that, or anything like that, on this weekday in March.
And the same goes for the fun
you might have gotten from group activities,
a likelihood attributed to everyone under your sign.

A dramatic rise in income may be a reason
to treat yourself, but that would apply
more to all the Pisces who are still alive,
still swimming up and down the stream of life
or suspended in a pool in the shade of an overhanging tree.

But you will be relieved to learn
that you no longer need to reflect carefully before acting
nor do you have to think more of others,
and never again will creative work take a back seat
to the business responsibilities that you never really had.

And don't worry today or any day
about problems caused by your unwillingness
to interact rationally with your many associates.
No more goals for you, no more romance,
no more money or children, jobs or important tasks,
but then again, you were never thus encumbered.

So leave it up to me now
to plan carefully for success and the wealth it may bring,
to value the dear ones close to my heart,
and to welcome any intellectual stimulation that comes my way
though that sounds like a lot to get done on a Tuesday.

I am better off closing the newspaper,
putting on the same clothes I wore yesterday
(when I read that your financial prospects were looking up)
then pushing off on my copper-colored bicycle
and pedaling along the shore road by the bay.

And you stay just as you are,
lying there in your beautiful blue suit,
your hands crossed on your chest

like the wings of a bird who has flown
in its strange migration not north or south
but straight up from earth
and pierced the enormous circle of the zodiac.

Hell

I have a feeling that it is much worse
than shopping for a mattress at a mall,

of greater duration without question,
and there is no random pitchforking here,
no licking flames to fear,
only this cavernous store with its maze of bedding.

Yet wandering past the jovial kings,
the more sensible queens,
and the cheerless singles
no satin sheet will ever cover,

I am thinking of a passage from the *Inferno,*
which I could fully bring to mind
and recite in English or even Italian

if the salesman who has been following us—
a crumpled pack of Newports
visible in the pocket of his short sleeve shirt—
would stop insisting for a moment
that we test this one, then this softer one,

which we do by lying down side by side,
arms rigid, figures on a tomb,
powerless to imagine what it would be like

to sleep or love this way
under the punishing rows of fluorescent lights,
which Dante would have surely included
had he lain on his back between us here today.

A Question About Birds

I am going to sit on a rock near some water
or on a slope of grass
under a high ceiling of white clouds,

and I am going to stop talking
so I can wander around in that spot
the way John Audubon might have wandered

through a forest of speckled sunlight,
stopping now and then to lean
against an elm, mop his brow,

and listen to the songs of birds.
Did he wonder, as I often do,
how they regard the songs of other species?

Would it be like listening to the Chinese
merchants at an outdoor market?
Or do all the birds perfectly understand one another?

Or is that nervous chittering
I often hear from the upper branches
the sound of some tireless little translator?

Watercoloring

The sky began to tilt,
a shift of light toward the higher clouds,
so I seized my brush
and dipped my little cup in the stream,

but once I streaked the paper gray
with a hint of green,
water began to slide down the page,
rivulets looking for a river.

And again, I was too late—
then the sky made another turn,
this time as if to face a mirror
held in the outstretched arm of a god.

Poem on the Three Hundredth Anniversary of the Trinity School

When a man asked me to look back three hundred years
Over the hilly landscape of America,
I must have picked up the wrong pen,
The one that had no poem lurking in its vein of ink.

So I walked in circles for days like a blind horse
Harnessed to an oaken pole that turns a millstone,
A sight we might have seen so many years ago—
Barley being ground near a swift and silent millrace—

Which led to other sights of smoky battlefields,
The frames of houses, then a tall steeple by a thoroughfare,
Which I climbed and then could see even more,
A nation being built of logs and words, ideas, and wooden nails.

The greatest of my grandfathers was not visible,
And the house I live in was not a pasture yet,
Only a wooded hillside strewn with glacial rock,
Yet I could see Dutch men and women on an island without bridges.

And I saw winding through the scene a line of people,
Students it would seem from their satchels and jackets,
Three hundred of them, one for every school year
Walking single-file over the decades into the present.

I thought of the pages they had filled
With letters and numbers, the lifted bits of chalk,
The changing flag limp in the corner, the hand raised,
The learning eye brightening to a spark in the iris.

And then I heard their singing, all those voices
Joined in a fluid chorus, and all those years
Synchronized by the harmony of their anthem,
History now a single chord, and time its key and measure.

The Chairs That No One Sits In

You see them on porches and on lawns
down by the lakeside,
usually arranged in pairs implying a couple

who might sit there and look out
at the water or the big shade trees.
The trouble is you never see anyone

sitting in these forlorn chairs
though at one time it must have seemed
a good place to stop and do nothing for a while.

Sometimes there is a little table
between the chairs where no one
is resting a glass or placing a book facedown

It may not be any of my business,
but let us suppose one day
that everyone who placed those vacant chairs

on a veranda or a dock sat down in them
if only for the sake of remembering
what it was they thought deserved

to be viewed from two chairs,
side by side with a table in between.
The clouds are high and massive on that day.

The woman looks up from her book.
The man takes a sip of his drink.
Then there is only the sound of their looking,

the lapping of lake water, and a call of one bird
then another, cries of joy or warning—
it passes the time to wonder which.

Memorizing "The Sun Rising" by John Donne

Every reader loves the way he tells off
the sun, shouting busy old fool
into the English skies even though they
were likely cloudy on that seventeenth-century morning.

And it's a pleasure to spend this sunny day
pacing the carpet and repeating the words,
feeling the syllables lock into rows
until I can stand and declare,
the book held closed by my side,
that hours, days, and months are but the rags of time.

But after a few steps into stanza number two,
wherein the sun is blinded by his mistress's eyes,
I can feel the first one begin to fade
like the puffs of sky-written letters on a windy day.

And by the time I have taken in the third,
the second is likewise gone, a blown-out candle now,
a wavering line of acrid smoke.

So it's not until I leave the house
and walk three times around this hidden lake
that the poem begins to show
any interest in walking by my side.

Then, after my circling,
better than the courteous dominion
of her being all states and him all princes,

better than love's power to shrink
the wide world to the size of a bedchamber,

and better even than the compression
of all that into the rooms of these three stanzas

is how, after hours stepping up and down the poem,
testing the plank of every line,
it goes with me now, contracted into a little spot within.

My Unborn Children

> . . . of all your children,
> only those who were born.
>
> —Wislawa Szymborska

I have so many of them I sometimes lose track,
several hundred last time I counted
but that was years ago.

I remember one was made of marble
and another looked like a goose
some days and on other days a white flower.

Many of them appeared only in dreams
or while I was writing a poem
with freezing fingers in the house of a miser.

Others were more like me,
looking out the window in a worn shirt
then later staring into the dark.

None of them ever made the lacrosse team,
but they all made me as proud
as I was on the day they failed to be born.

There is no telling—
maybe tonight or later in the week
another one of my children will not be born.

I see this next one as a baby
lying naked below a ceiling pasted with stars
but only for a little while,

then I see him as a monk in a gray robe
walking back and forth
in the gravel yard of an imaginary monastery,

his head bowed, wondering where I am.

Hangover

If I were crowned emperor this morning,
every child who is playing Marco Polo
in the swimming pool of this motel,
shouting the name Marco Polo back and forth

Marco   Polo   Marco   Polo

would be required to read a biography
of Marco Polo—a long one with fine print—
as well as a history of China and of Venice,
the birthplace of the venerated explorer

Marco   Polo   Marco   Polo

after which each child would be quizzed
by me then executed by drowning
regardless how much they managed
to retain about the glorious life and times of

Marco   Polo   Marco   Polo

Table Talk

Not long after we had sat down to dinner
at a long table in a restaurant in Chicago
and were deeply engrossed in the heavy menus,
one of us—a bearded man with a colorful tie—
asked if anyone had ever considered
applying the paradoxes of Zeno to the martyrdom of St. Sebastian.

The differences between these two figures
were much more striking than the differences
between the Cornish hen and the trout amandine
I was wavering between, so I looked up and closed my menu.

If, the man with the tie continued,
an object moving through space
will never reach its destination because it is always
limited to cutting the distance to its goal in half,

then it turns out that St. Sebastian did not die
from the wounds inflicted by the arrows:
the cause of death was fright at the spectacle of their approach.
Saint Sebastian, according to Zeno, would have died of a heart attack.

I think I'll have the trout, I told the waiter
for it was now my turn to order,
but all through the elegant dinner
I kept thinking of the arrows forever nearing

the pale, quivering flesh of St. Sebastian
a fleet of them forever halving the tiny distances
to his body, tied to post with rope,
even after the archers had packed it in and gone home.

And I thought of the bullet never reaching
the wife of William Burroughs, an apple trembling on her head,
the tossed acid never getting to the face of that girl,
and the Oldsmobile never knocking my dog into a ditch.

The theories of Zeno floated above the table
like thought balloons from the 5th century before Christ,
yet my fork continued to arrive at my mouth
delivering morsels of asparagus and crusted fish,

and after we ate and lifted our glasses,
we left the restaurant and said goodbye on the street
then walked our separate ways in the world where things do arrive,

where people usually get where they are going—
where trains pull into the station in a cloud of vapor,
where geese land with a splash on the surface of a pond,
and the one you love crosses the room and arrives in your arms—

and, yes, where sharp arrows can pierce a torso,
splattering blood on the groin and the feet of the saint,

that popular subject of European religious painting.
One hagiographer compared him to a hedgehog bristling with quills.

Delivery

Moon in the upper window,
shadow of my crooked pen on the page,
and I find myself wishing that the news of my death

might be delivered not by a dark truck
but by a child's attempt to draw that truck—
the long rectangular box of the trailer,

some lettering on the side,
then the protruding cab, the ovoid wheels,
maybe the inscrutable profile of a driver,

and puffs of white smoke
issuing from the tailpipe, drawn like flowers
and similar in their expression to the clouds in the sky, only smaller.

What She Said

When he told me he expected me to pay for dinner,
I was like give me a break.

I was not the exact equivalent of give me a break.
I was just similar to give me a break.

As I said, I was like give me a break.

I would love to tell you
how I was able to resemble give me a break
without actually being identical to give me a break,

but all I can say is that I sensed
a similarity between me and give me a break.

And that was close enough
at that point in the evening

even if it meant I would fall short
of standing up from the table and screaming
Give me a break,

for God's sake will you please give me a break?!

No, for that moment
with the rain streaking the restaurant windows
and the waiter approaching,

I felt the most I could be was like

to a certain degree

give me a break.

Drawing You from Memory

I seem to have forgotten several features
crucial to the doing of this,
for instance, how your lower lip
meets your upper lip besides just being below it,
and what happens at the end of the nose,
how much does it shade the plane of your cheek,
and would even a bit of nostril be visible from this angle?
Chinese eyes, you call them
which could be the difficulty I have
in showing the flash of light in your iris,
and being so far away from you for so long,
I cannot remember what direction
it flows, the deep river of your hair.

But all of this will come together
the minute I see you again at the station,
my notebook and pens packed away,
your face smiling as I cup it in my hands,
or frowning later when we are home
and you are berating me in the kitchen
waving the pages in my face
demanding to know the name of this latest little whore.

Cemetery Ride

My new copper-colored bicycle
is looking pretty fine under a blue sky
as I pedal along one of the sandy paths
in the Palm Cemetery here in Florida,

wheeling past the headstones of the Lyons,
the Campbells, the Dunlaps, and the Davenports,
Arthur and Ethel, who outlived him by 11 years
I slow down even more to notice,

but not so much as to fall sideways on the ground.
And here's a guy named Happy Grant
next to his wife Jean in their endless bed.
Annie Sue Simms is right there and sounds

a lot more fun than Theodosia S. Hawley.
And good afternoon, Emily Polasek
and to you too, George and Jane Cooper,
facing each other in profile, two sides of a coin.

I wish I could take you all for a ride
in my wire basket on this glorious April day,
not a thing as simple as your name, Bill Smith,
even trickier then Clarence Augustus Coddington.

Then how about just you, Enid Parker?
Would you like to gather up your voluminous skirts
and ride side-saddle on the crossbar
and tell me what happened between 1863 and 1931?

I'll even let you ring the silver bell.
But if you're not ready, I can always ask
Mary Brennan to rise from her long sleep
beneath the swaying grey beards of Spanish moss

and ride with me along these halls of the dead
so I can listen to her strange laughter
as some crows flap overhead in the blue
and the spokes of my wheels catch the dazzling sun.

Lakeside

As optical illusions go
it was one of the more spectacular,
a cluster of bright stars
appearing to move across the night sky
as if on a secret mission

while, of course, it was the low clouds
that were doing the moving,
scattered over my head by a wind from the east.
And as hard as I looked
I could not get the stars to budge again.

It was like the curious figure
of the duck/rabbit—
why, even paradoxical Wittgenstein
could not find his way back to the rabbit
once he had beheld the bill of the duck.

But which was which?
Were the stars the rabbit
and the blown clouds the duck?
or the other way around?
You're being ridiculous,

I said to myself,
on the walk back to the house,
but then the correct answer struck me
not like a bolt of lightning,
but more like a heavy bolt of cloth.

My Hero

Just as the hare is zipping across the finish line,
the tortoise has stopped once again
by the roadside,
this time to stick out his neck
and nibble a bit of sweet grass,
unlike the previous time
when he was distracted
by a bee humming in the heart of a wildflower.

Poetry Workshop Held in a
Former Cigar Factory in Key West

After our final class, when we disbanded
as the cigar rollers here had disbanded decades ago,
getting up from their benches for the last time
as the man who read to them during their shift
closed his book without marking the page where he left off,
I complimented myself on my restraint.

For never in that sunny white building
did I draw an analogy between cigar-making and poetry.
Not even after I had studied the display case
containing the bladed *chaveta,* the ring gauge,
and the hand guillotine with its measuring rule
did I suggest that the cigar might be a model for the poem.

Nor did I ever cite the exemplary industry
of those anonymous rollers and cutters –
the best producing 300 cigars in a day
compared to 3 flawless poems in a lifetime if you're lucky—
who worked the broad leaves of tobacco
into cylinders ready to be held lightly in the hand.

Not once did I imply that tightly rolling an intuition
into a perfectly shaped, hand-made thing

might encourage a reader to remove the brightly colored
encircling band and slip it over her finger
and take the poet as her spouse in a sudden puff of smoke.
No, I kept all of that to myself, until now.

Returning the Pencil to Its Tray

Everything is fine—
the first bits of sun are on
the yellow flowers behind the low wall,

people in cars are on their way to work,
and I will never have to write again.

Just looking around
will suffice from here on in.

Who said I had to always play
the secretary of the interior?

And I am getting good at being blank,
staring at all the zeroes in the air.

It must have been all the time spent
in the kayak this summer
that brought this out,

the yellow one which went
nicely with the pale blue life jacket—

the sudden, tippy
buoyancy of the launch,

then the exertion, striking
into the wind against the short waves,

but the best was drifting back,
the paddle resting athwart the craft,
and me mindless in the middle of time.

Not even that dark cormorant
perched on the *No Wake* sign,
his narrow head raised
as if he were looking over something,

not even that inquisitive little fellow
could bring me to write another word.

NEW POEMS

The Sandhill Cranes of Nebraska

Too bad you weren't here six months ago,
was a lament I heard on my visit to Nebraska.
You could have seen the astonishing spectacle
of the sandhill cranes, thousands of them
feeding and even dancing on the shores of the Platte River.

There was no point in pointing out
the impossibility of my being there then
because I happened to be somewhere else,
so I nodded and put on a look of mild disappointment
if only to be part of the commiseration.

It was the same look I remember wearing
about six months ago in Georgia
when I was told that I had just missed
the spectacular annual outburst of azaleas,
brilliant against the green backdrop of spring

and the same in Vermont six months before that
when I arrived shortly after
the magnificent foliage had gloriously peaked,
Mother Nature, as she is called,
having touched the hills with her many-colored brush,

a phenomenon that occurs, like the others,
around the same time every year when I am apparently off
in another state, stuck in a motel lobby
with the local paper and a styrofoam cup of coffee,
busily missing God knows what.

Foundling

How unusual to be living a life of continual self-expression,
jotting down little things,
noticing a leaf being carried down a stream,
then wondering what will become of me,

and finally to work alone under a lamp
as if everything depended on this,
groping blindly down a page,
like someone lost in a forest.

And to think it all began one night
on the steps of a nunnery
where I lay gazing up from a sewing basket,
which was doubling for a proper baby carrier,

staring into the turbulent winter sky,
too young to wonder about anything
including my recent abandonment—
but it was there that I committed

my first act of self-expression,
sticking out my infant tongue
and receiving in return (I can see it now)
a large, pristine snowflake much like any other.

Catholicism

There's a possum who appears here at odd times,
often walking up the path to the house
in the middle of the day like a little ghost
with a long tail and a blank expression on his face.

He likes to slip behind the woodpile,
but sometimes he gets so close to the window
where I am standing with a glass in my hand
that I start to review my sins, systematically

going from one commandment to the next.
What is it about him that causes me
to begin an examination of conscience,
calling to mind my failings in this time of reflection?

It could just be the twitching of the tail
and that white face, but his slow priestly pace
also makes a contribution, as do the tiny paws,
more like hands, really, with opposable thumbs

able to carry a nut or dig a hole in the earth
or lift a chalice above his head
or even deliver a document,
I am thinking as he nears the back door,

not merely a subpoena but an order
of excommunication with my name and a date
written in fine Italian ink
and signed with a flourish of the papal sash.

Carrara

The Tyrrhenian Sea was bouncing off to the right
as we headed south down the coast,
and to the left rose the Apennine mountains,
some with their faces quarried away,
from where heavy blocks of white marble
had been cut and carried down
and stacked in rows in yards along the highway.

Is anyone hiding within? I wondered,
as we passed a little Fiat
and were passed in turn by a green Lamborghini,
hiding the way Pinocchio hid inside a log—
maybe a David who goes by another name,
or an anonymous girl caught dancing,
or any other figure encased and yet to be revealed.

Are you in there, Dawn with your sunburst halo,
concealed from the freshly sharpened chisel?
How about you, Spirit of Revolution
waving a flag of marble
and crushing the serpent of Tyranny with one foot?
Or is nobody home, no one barely breathing
in the heavy darkness of the pure white stone?

Soon, we were standing on a wide beach
where the body of Shelley had floated ashore,
and where all those questions washed away—
though later I pictured a sculptor wandering
among the blocks, hands clasped behind his back,
then deciding it was time to get to work
on a towering likeness of his favorite English poet.

Report from the Subtropics

For one thing, there's no more snow
to watch from an evening window,
and no armfuls of logs to carry into the house
so cumbersome you have to touch the latch with an elbow,

and once inside, no iron stove like an old woman
waiting to devour her early dinner of wood.

No hexagrams of frost to study
on the cold glass pages of the bathroom.

No black sweater to pull over my head
while I wait for the coffee to brew.

Instead, I walk around in children's clothes—
shorts and a tee shirt with the name of a band
lettered on the front, announcing me to nobody.

The sun never fails to arrive early
and refuses to leave the party
even after I go from room to room,
turning out all the lights, and making a face.

And the birds with those long white necks?
All they do is swivel their heads
keeping an eye on me as I walk along,
as if they all knew my password
and the name of the little town where I was born.

Lesson for the Day

I didn't know Marianne Moore
had written a little ode to a steam roller
until this morning. She has it walking
back and forth over the particles it has crushed.
She must have watched a lot of cartoons.
She also compares it to a butterfly unflatteringly.

I like it better when she speaks to a snail.
It's pleasurable to picture her in a garden
bending forward in her dated black clothes
and her tilted black triangle of a hat,
as she seriously addresses the fellow curled in its shell.

But when I see her standing before the big drum
of a steam roller and saying not very nice things,
only one eventuality ever comes to mind,
for I, too, am a serious student of cartoons.

And no one wants to avoid seeing
a flattened Marianne Moore hanging out to dry
on a clothesline or propped up
as a display in a store window more than I.

Promenade

As much as these erratic clouds keep sweeping
this way and that over the roof
of this blue house bordered by hedges and fruit trees,

and as much as the world continues to run
in all directions with its head in its hands,
there is one particular robin who appears

every morning on a section of lawn
by the front door with such regularity
he could be a lighthouse keeper or a clock maker.

He could be Immanuel Kant were he not so small
and feathered, whom the citizens set their watches by
as he walked through town with his hair curled.

It takes a lot to startle this bird—
only a hand clap will make him rise
to one of the low branches of the nearby apple tree.

So I am wondering if he would allow me
to slip a small collar around his neck
and take him for a walk, first around the house

then later, when more trust has been gained,
into town where we would pass the locals
with their children and orthodox dogs in tow,

and I would hold the robin lightly by a string
as we waited to cross the street, then he would hop
off the curb and off we would go

not caring about what people were saying
even when we stopped at a store front
to admire our strange reflections in the window.

The Unfortunate Traveler

Because I was off to France, I packed
my camera along with my shaving kit,
some colorful boxer shorts, and a sweater with a zipper,

but every time I tried to take a picture
of a bridge, a famous plaza,
or the bronze equestrian statue of a general,

there was a woman standing in front of me
taking a picture of the very same thing,
or the odd pedestrian blocked my view,

someone or something always getting between me
and the flying buttress, the river boat,
a bright café awning, an unexpected pillar.

So into the little door of the lens
came not the kiosk or the altarpiece.
No fresco or baptistry slipped by the quick shutter.

Instead, my memories of that glorious summer
of my youth are awakened now,
like an ember fanned into brightness,

by a shoulder, the back of a raincoat,
a wide hat or towering hairdo—
lost time miraculously recovered

by the buttons on a gendarme's coat
and my favorite,
the palm of that vigilant guard at the Louvre.

Drinking Alone

after Li Po

This is not after Li Po
the way the state is after me
for neglecting to pay all my taxes,

nor the way I am after
the woman in front of me
on the long line at the post office.

Li Po, I am not saying
"After you"
as I stand holding open

one of the heavy glass doors
that divide the centuries
in a long corridor of glass doors.

No, the only way this is after you
is in the way they say
it's just one thing after another,

like the way I will pause
to raise a glass of wine to you
after I finish writing this poem.

So let me get back
to sitting in the wind alone
among the pines with a pencil in my hand.

After all, you had your turn,
and mine will soon be done
then someone else will sit here after me.

To My Favorite 17-Year-Old High School Girl

Do you realize that if you had started
building the Parthenon on the day you were born
you would be all done in only one more year?
Of course, you couldn't have done it alone,
so never mind, you're fine just as you are.
You are loved simply for being yourself.

But did you know that at your age Judy Garland
was pulling down $150,000 a picture,
Joan of Arc was leading the French army to victory,
and Blaise Pascal had cleaned up his room?
No wait, I mean he had invented the calculator.

Of course, there will be time for all that later in your life
after you come out of your room
and begin to blossom, or at least pick up all your socks

For some reason, I keep remembering that Lady Jane Grey
was Queen of England when she was only fifteen,
but then she was beheaded, so never mind her as a role model.

A few centuries later, when he was your age,
Franz Schubert was doing the dishes for his family
but that did not keep him from composing two symphonies,
four operas, and two complete Masses as a youngster.

But of course that was in Austria at the height
of romantic lyricism, not here in the suburbs of Cleveland.

Frankly, who cares if Annie Oakley was a crack shot at 15
or if Maria Callas debuted as Tosca at 17?

We think you are special by just being you,
playing with your food and staring into space.
By the way, I lied about Schubert doing the dishes,
but that doesn't mean he *never* helped out around the house.

Animal Behavior

Among the animals who avoid danger
just by being still,
the heron is a favorite example,
indistinguishable from the reeds
he stands in, thin and gray, at the water's edge.

Then there is the snowy egret
who must think he can make
his white question mark of a body
just vanish from the lake
by being as motionless as can be.

And when it comes to people
there's the quiet man at the bar
who lifts his eyes only now and then
as well as the girl in the summer dress
who must pretend she is not here.

And who am I to talk,
the last flamingo to leave the party,
good at avoiding danger so far,
away from any cove or shore,
conspicuous as the drink I carry out the door.

Lincoln

Whatever it was that just flew out of my head
did not leave a trace,
not a contrail in the sky
not a footprint in a field of new snow.

The last thing I remember
is reading a sentence
in a long biography of Abraham Lincoln,
something about his face being so ugly

it became beautiful
in the eyes of Walt Whitman,
but there was something after
that made me fold down the corner

of the page and close the book—
so much I cannot think of today,
a team of white birds lifting off a shoreline
and disappearing into the sun.

Note to Antonín Dvořák

Maestro, I am writing to tell you
that your serenade in D minor
with its stretches of martial confidence
then some sweet wanderings of the woodwinds

has not really brought me to the edge of anything,
yet compared to the inane movie
being shown on this long flight to Seattle,
listening to your music has made me a better

person than that other self,
so slack of jaw and fishy of stare,
who would have watched the movie to its end
oblivious to the startling 33,000 feet of air below.

I never visited your tomb in Prague
or even the site of your former apartment
on East 17th Street before it was demolished
to make room for a hospital for sufferers from AIDS.

So I am thanking you here for the lift
of a tune to ride with over the clouds
high above towns bisected by roads,
and fields with their plowed circles.

You remind me of a canary
I once stared at for an unusually long time
and the communion that developed between us
as we gazed into and out of the unhooded cage.

Time well spent, I thought,
as the bird broke it off and began to peck
at the image of his twin in a little oval mirror,
leaving me to return to the many ways

we have concocted to waste our lives—
ten thousand at least, wouldn't you say,
Maestro, with your baton, your furious pencil,
and the closet where all your dark clothes used to hang.

Sunday Walk

Not only colorful beds of flowers
ruffled today by a breeze off the lake
but the ruffled surface of the lake itself,
and later a boathouse and an oak tree
so old its heavy limbs rested on the ground.

And I don't want to leave out
the uniformed campus guard I saw studying
a map of the campus without a student in sight.

Closer to town, shops under awnings
and several churches,
one topped with a burnished cross,
another announcing a sermon:
"What You *Can* Take with You."

So many odd things to see
but mostly it's the sun at its apex
inscribing little circles,
little haloes at the top of the sky,
and the freshening breeze,
the nowhere it came from
and the nowhere it is headed,
every leaf wavering, each branch bowed,

and what can I do, I heard myself asking,
with all this evidence of something,
me without a candle, wafer, or a rug,
not even a compass to tell me which way to face.

The Suggestion Box

It all began fairly early in the day
at the coffee shop as it turned out
when the usual waitress said
I'll bet you're going to write a poem about this
after she had knocked a cup of coffee into my lap.

Then later in the morning I was told
by a student that I should write a poem
about the fire drill that was going on
as we all stood on the lawn outside our building.

In the afternoon a woman I barely knew
said you could write a poem about that,
pointing to a dirigible that was passing overhead.

And if all that were not enough,
a friend turned to me as we walked past
a man whose face was covered with tattoos
and said, I see a poem coming!

Why is everyone being so helpful?
I wondered that evening by the shore of a lake.

Maybe I should write a poem
about all the people who think
they know what I should be writing poems about.

It was just then in the fading light that I spotted
a pair of ducks emerging
from a cluster of reeds to paddle out to open water,

the female glancing back over her russet shoulder
just in time to see me searching my pockets for a pen.

I knew it, she quacked, with a bit of a brogue.
But who can blame you for following your heart?
she went on.
Now, go write a lovely poem about me and the mister.

Cheerios

One bright morning in a restaurant in Chicago
as I waited for my eggs and toast,
I opened the *Tribune* only to discover
that I was the same age as Cheerios.

Indeed, I was a few months older than Cheerios
for today, the newspaper announced,
was the seventieth birthday of Cheerios
whereas mine had occurred earlier in the year.

Already I could hear them whispering
behind my stooped and threadbare back,
Why that dude's older than Cheerios
the way they used to say

Why that's as old as the hills,
only the hills are much older than Cheerios
or any American breakfast cereal,
and more noble and enduring are the hills,

I surmised as a bar of sunlight illuminated my orange juice.

Quandary

I was a little disappointed
in the apple I lifted from a bowl of fruit
and bit into on the way out the door,
fuzzy on the inside and lacking the snap of the ripe.

Yesterday it was probably perfect,
I figured, as I held it out before me,
soft red apple bearing my tooth marks,
as if I were contemplating the bust of Aristotle.

I considered all the people
who would be grateful to have this apple,
and others who might find it in their hearts
to kill me before slipping it into a pocket.

And I considered another slice
of the world's population, too,
those who are shielded from anything
as offensive as a slightly imperfect apple.

Then I took a second bite, a big one,
and pitched what was left
over the tall hedges hoping to hit on the head
a murderer or one of the filthy rich out for a stroll.

Elusive

As I was wandering the city this morning
working on my impression of Michael Caine,
I began to think about her again—

which makes it sound as if she were far away
or lost in the past or possibly both.

But I was with her only an hour ago,
and later I will sit in the kitchen
and watch her hair hiding her face

as she stirs some onions and butter in a skillet
and I pour us a glass of frosty white wine.

Still, she has been known to vanish
as if in a mist as we walk past
a row of store windows, or she will disappear

behind a hedge or into a side room at a party.
And often no aisle of the supermarket reveals her.

Like the fox, she is nowhere and everywhere,
a tail of fire out of the corner of my eye,
one of the corners she likes to turn

just as the streetlights are coming on
when I am searching for her in the evening crowd.

Would she and Michael Caine hit it off,
I wondered as I emerged from an alley
only to see her staring at me from a spot on a public bench.

Looking for a Friend in a Crowd of Arriving Passengers: A Sonnet

Not John Whalen.
Not John Whalen.
Not John Whalen.
Not John Whalen.
Not John Whalen.
Not John Whalen.
Not John Whalen.
Not John Whalen.
Not John Whalen.
Not John Whalen.
Not John Whalen.
Not John Whalen.
Not John Whalen.
John Whalen.

Digging

It seems whenever I dig in the woods
on the slope behind this house
I unearth some object from the past—
a shard of crockery or a bottle with its stopper missing,

sometimes a piece of metal, maybe handled
by the dairy farmer who built this house
over a century and a half ago
as civil war waged unabated to the south.

So it's never a surprise
when the shovel-tip hits a rusted bolt,
or a glass knob from a drawer—
little hands waving from the past.

And today, it's a buried toy,
a little car with a dent in the roof
and enough flecks of paint to tell it was blue.
Shrouded in a towel, the body of our cat

lies nearby on the ground where I settled her
in the mottled light of the summer trees,
and I still have to widen the hole
and deepen it for her by at least another foot,

but not before I stop for a moment
with the once-blue car idling in my palm,
to imagine the boy who grew up here
and to see that two of the crusted wheels still spin.

Central Park

It's hard to describe how that day in the park
was altered when I stopped to read
an official sign I came across near the great carousel,
my lips moving silently like the lips of Saint Ambrose.

As the carousel turned in the background,
all pinions and mirrors and the heads of horses
rising to the steam-blown notes of a calliope,
I was learning how the huge thing
was first designed to be powered
by a blind mule, as it turned out,
strapped to the oar of a wheel in an earthen
room directly below the merry turning of the carousel.

The sky did not darken with this news
nor did a general silence fall on the strollers
or the ball players on the green fields.
No one even paused to look my way,
though I must have looked terrible
as I stood there filling with sympathy
not so much for the harnessed beast
tediously making its rounds,

but instead for the blind mule within me
always circling in the dark—
the mule who makes me turn when my name is called
or causes me to nod with a wooden gaze
or sit doing nothing on a bench in the shape of a swan.

Somewhere, there must still be a door
to that underground room,
the lock rusted shut, the iron key misplaced,
last year's leaves piled up against the sill,
and inside, a trace of straw on the floor,
a whiff of manure, and maybe a forgotten bit
or a bridle hanging from a hook in the dark.

Poor blind beast, I sang softly as I left the park,
poor blind me, poor blind earth turning blindly on its side.

Osprey

Oh, large brown, thickly feathered creature
with a distinctive white head,
you, perched on the top branch
of a tree near the lake shore,

as soon as I guide this boat back to the dock
and walk up the grassy path to the house,
before I unzip my windbreaker
and lift the binoculars from around my neck,

before I wash the gasoline from my hands,
before I tell anyone I'm back,
and before I hang the ignition key on its nail,
or pour myself a drink—

I'm thinking a vodka soda with lemon—
I will look you up in my
illustrated guide to North American birds
and I promise I will learn what you are called.

Here and There

I feel nothing this morning
except the low hum of the ego,
a constant, shameless sound behind the rib cage.

I even keep forgetting my friend in surgery
at this very hour.

In other words, a perfect time to write
about clouds rolling in after a week of sun
and a woman beating laundry on a rock
in front of her house overlooking the sea—

all of which I am making up—
the clouds, the house, the woman, even the laundry.

Or take the lights strung in a line line
that I once saw from the bow of a sailboat,
which seemed unreal at the time and more unreal now.

Even if I were there again at the ship's railing
as I am sitting here in a lawn chair, who would believe it?

Vast maple tree above me, are you really there?
and you, open cellar door,
and you, vast sky with sun and a fading contrail—

no more real than the pretend city
where she lies now under the investigating lights,
an imaginary surgeon busy
breaking into the vault of her phantom skull.

Villanelle

The first line will not go away
though the middle ones will disappear,
and the third, like the first, is bound to get more play.

Examples of this type are written every day,
and whether uplifting or drear,
that first line will just not go away.

It seems some lines have the right of way.
It's their job to reappear,
for example, the third, designed to get more play.

Whether you squawk like an African Grey
or sing sweetly to the inner ear,
the line you wrote first will just not go away.

You may compose all night and day
under a bare lightbulb or a crystal chandelier,
but line number three must get more play.

How can a poet hope to go wildly astray
or sing out like a romantic gondolier
when the first line will not go away
and the third always has the final say?

Lines Written at Flying Point Beach

or at least in the general vicinity
of Flying Point Beach,
certainly closer than I normally am

to that beach where the ocean
crests the dunes at high tide
spilling tons of new salt water into Mecox Bay,

and probably closer to Flying Point Beach
than you are right now
or I happen to be as you read this.

But how close do I really need to be
to Flying Point Beach
or to any beach in order to write these lines?

Oh, Flying Point Beach,
I love all three words in your name,
not to mention the deep, white sand

and the shorebirds on their thin legs
facing into the wind
along that low stretch between the ocean and the bay.

How satisfying it is to be
even within bicycling distance of you,
though it's dangerous to ride at the edge of these roads.

Thoreau had his cabin near a pond.
Virginia Woolf stood on the shore of the River Ouse,
and here I am writing all this down

not very far at all—maybe twenty minutes by taxi
if the driver ever manages to find this place—
from the many natural wonders of Flying Point Beach.

Lines Written in a Garden by a
Cottage in Herefordshire

No, this time I'm not kidding around.
There's some half-shattered outdoor furniture,
then crowds of dianthus and pink hydrangeas,
honeysuckle going wild over the bright blue door,
and zinc buckets and coal carriers overflowing
with pansies, lavender, and some kind of soft fern—
just the right combination of growth and neglect.

And you don't have to wish for a brick wall,
a gravel path or a leaning disused shed
to complete the picture because they're all right here
as well as a concrete statue of a maiden
holding a jug, one breast exposed, overgrown with ivy.
The only thing you might not think of,
being in another place so far away,

is this one bee who just refused to wait
for all the morning glories to unfurl in the early sun,
and instead, pushed her way into the white flute
of a blossom, disappearing for a moment
before she flew off in her distinctive gold
and black uniform like a player on a team,
heading over the hedge toward a core of honey.

American Airlines #371

Pardon my benevolence,
but given the illusion that my fellow passengers and I
are now on our way to glory,
rising over this kingdom of clouds
(airy citadels! unnamable goings-on within!)
and at well over 500 miles per hour,
which would get you to work in under one second,

I wish to forgive the man next to me
who so annoyed me before the wine started arriving
by turning each page of his newspaper
with a kind of crisp, military snap,
and the same goes for that howling infant,
and for the child in the row behind me
who persisted in hitting that F above high C
that all of her kind know perfectly how to hit
while rhythmically kicking the back of my seat.

Yes, I have softened and been rendered
even grateful by the ministrations of Eva,
uniformed wine bearer in the sky,
and if we are not exactly being conveyed to Paradise,
at least we are vectoring across the continent
to Los Angeles—orange tree in the backyard,
girl on a motorcycle roaring down Venice Boulevard.

And eventually we will begin our final descent
(*final descent!* I want to shout to Eva)
into the city of a million angels,
where the world might terminate or begin afresh again,
which is how I tend to feel almost every day—

life's end just around another corner or two,
yet out the morning window
the thrust of a new blossom from that bush
whose colorful name I can never remember.

Keats: or How I Got My Negative Capability Back

I remember the first time I realized
how lacking I was in Negative Capability.
It was on a long slope of lawn
next to a turreted stone building
that housed the shenanigans
of the department of English.

Some brown birds were pecking in the grass,
and yet here I was, a nineteen year old
too concerned with my clothes
and the nervous mystery of girls
to identify with this group of common sparrows
another student was pointing to,
let alone the nightingale we had read about,
invisible in the woods of England.

I was so short on empathy in those days
the only Negative Capability I could have possessed
would be negative Negative Capability,
which I could have turned into a positive
had Keats not so firmly determined
that regular Negative Capability was already a positive thing.

All those birds are surely dead by now,
no more hopping around
in the grass of Massachusetts for them,

but I'm still here this afternoon
looking at a dog asleep half under the porch,
an old brown mongrel with a hoary muzzle,
his paws twitching so frantically
I can even see what he is dreaming
as the sun helps itself down the sky.
Yes, I am watching him jump a stone wall
in pursuit of a darting rabbit—
I'm way up on a high branch
of a tree that is swaying in the wind of his dream.

The Music of the Spheres

The woman on the radio
who was lodging the old complaint
that her husband never listens to her

reminded me of the music of the spheres,
that chord of seven notes,
one for each of the visible planets,

which has been sounding
since the beginning of the universe,
and which we can never hear,

according to Pythagoras
because we hear it all the time
so it sounds the same as silence.

But let's say the needle were lifted
from the spinning grooves
of those celestial orbs—

then people would stop
on the streets and look up,
and others would stop in the fields

and hikers would stop in the woods
and look this way and that
as if they were hearing something

for the first time,
and that husband would lower
the newspaper from his face

look at his wife
who has been standing in the doorway
and ask *Did you just say something, dear?*

Orient

You are turning me
like someone turning a globe in her hand,
and yes, I have another side
like a China no one,
not even me, has ever seen.

So describe to me what's there,
say what you are looking at
and I will close my eyes
so I can see it too,
the oxcarts and all the lively flags.

I love the sound of your voice
like a little saxophone
telling me what I could never know
unless I dug a hole all the way down
through the core of my self.

Heraclitus on Vacation

It is possible to stick your foot
into the same swimming pool twice,

dive, or even cannonball
into the deep or shallow end

as many times as you like
depending on how much you had to drink.

Ode to a Desk Lamp

Oh faithful light, under which I have written
and read for all these decades,
flying saucer with your underbelly softly aglow,
rising on a stem from a heavy metal base,

lamp I rescued from my old girlfriend's mother,
who was about to toss you
from her condo on a bluff
overlooking the ruffled Pacific.

Has anyone been with me longer?
me without siblings or children,
you with your kindly 60 watt frosted bulb,
you who have not died like others I knew,

you nestled in a bath towel
on the floorboards of the car
as I backed it down the driveway of my marriage
and steered east then south down the two- then four-lane roads.

So may nights like this one,
me sleepless, you gazing down on the page
and now on a crystal rock, a tiny figure of a pig,
and an orchid dying in its blue China pot.

But that is more than enough
of the sad drapery of the past as I hold the present
between two fingers and the thumb
and a blue train whistles in the distance.

It's time to saddle up, partner,
once I unplug your tail from the socket,
time to ride out west,
far from the gaucheries of men,

the inconstancy of women,
and the rowdy mortality of them all,
until we find a grove of trees near a river—
just you and me with our bedrolls under a scattering of stars.

Irish Poetry

That morning under a pale hood of sky
I heard the unambiguous scrape of spackling
against the side of our wickered, penitential house.

The day mirled and clabbered
in the thick, stony light,
and the rooks' feathered narling
astounded the salt waves, the plush arm of coast.

I carried my bucket past the forked
coercion of a tree, up toward
the pious and nictitating preeminence of a school,
hunkered there in its gully of learning.

But only later, as I stood before a wash-stand
and gaunt, phosphorescent heifers
swam purposefully beyond these windows
did the whorled and sparky gib of the indefinite
manage to whorl me into knowledge.

Then, I heard the ghost-clink of milk bottle
on the rough threshold
and understood the meadow-bells
that trembled over a nimbus of ragwort—
the whole afternoon lambent, corrugated, puddle-mad.

After the Funeral

When you told me you needed a *drink*-drink
and not just a drink like a drink of water,

I steered you by the elbow into a corner bar,
which turned out to be a real *bar*-bar,

dim and nearly empty with little tables in the back
where we drank and agreed that the funeral

was a real *funeral*-funeral complete with a Mass,
incense, and tons of eulogies.

You know, I always considered Tom a real
friend-friend, you said, lifting your *drink*-drink

to your lips, and I agreed that Tom
was much more than just an ordinary friend.

We also concurred that Angela's black dress
was elegant but not like *elegant*-elegant,

just elegant enough. And a few hours later
when the bartender brought yet another round

of whiskeys to our table in the corner
we recognized by his apron and his mighty girth

that he was more than just a bartender.
A true *bartender*-bartender was what he was

we decided, with a respectful *clink*-clink
of our *drink*-drinks, amber in a chink of afternoon light.

Best Fall

was what we called a game we played
which had nothing to do
with a favorite autumn,
somebody else's gorgeous reds and yellows.

no, eleven years old
all we wanted was to be shot
as we charged sacrificially into the fire
of the shooter lying prone behind a hedge

or even better, to be that shooter
and pick off the others
as they charged the gun
each one stopping in his young tracks

to writhe and twist
aping the contortions of death
from the movies,
clutching our bleeding hearts

holding ourselves
as we lifted—a moment of ballet—
into the air then tumbled
into the grass behind our houses.

and whoever invented that game
made sure it would have
no ending,
for the one who was awarded

best fall by the shooter
got to be the next shooter
and so it went, shooting and being shot,
tearing at our cowboy shirts

trying our best
to make death look good
until it got almost dark
and our mothers called us in.

France

You and your frozen banana,
you and your crème brûlée.
Can't we just skip dessert
and go back to the Hotel d'Orsay?

You and your apple tart
and your plates of profiteroles.
Can't we just ask for the check?
Can't you hear Time's mortal call?

Why linger here at the table
stuffing ourselves with sweets
when all the true pleasures await us
in room trois cent quarante-huit?

All Eyes

Just because I'm dead now doesn't mean
I don't exist anymore.
All those eulogies and the obituary
in the corner of the newspaper
have made me feel more vibrant than ever.

I'm here in some fashion,
maybe like a gust of wind
that disturbs the upper leaves,
or blows a hat around a corner,
or disperses a little cloud of mayflies over a stream.

What I like best about this
is you realizing you can no longer
get away with things the way you used to
when it would be ten o'clock at night
and I wouldn't know where you were.

I'm all ears, you liked to say
whenever you couldn't bother listening.
And now you know that I'm all eyes,
looking in every direction,
and a special eye is always trained on you.

Rome in June

There was a lot to notice that morning
in the Church of Saint Dorothy, virgin martyr—

a statue of Mary with a halo of electric lights,
a faded painting of a saint in flight,
Joseph of Copertino, as it turned out,
and an illustration above a side altar
bearing the title "The Musical Ecstasy of St. Francis."

But what struck me in a special way
like a pebble striking the forehead
was the realization that the simple design
running up the interior of the church's dome

was identical to the design on the ceiling
of the room by the Spanish Steps
where Keats had died and where I
had stood with lifted eyes just the day before.

It was nothing more than a row
of squares, each with the carved head
of a white flower on a background of blue,

but all during the priest's sermon
(which was either about the Wedding at Cana
or the miracle of the loaves and fishes
as far as my Italian could tell)
I was staring at the same image
that the author of *Hyperion* had stared at
from his death bed as he was being devoured by tuberculosis.

It was worth coming to Rome
if only to see what supine Keats was beholding
just before there would be no more Keats,
only Shelley, not yet swallowed by a wave,
and Byron before his Greek fever,
and Wordsworth who outlived Romanticism itself.

And it pays to lift the eyes, I thought outside the church
where a man on a bench was reading a newspaper,
a woman was scolding her child,
and the heavy sky, visible above the narrow streets
of Trastevere, was in the process
of breaking up, showing segments of blue
and the occasional flash of Roman sunlight.

The Deep

Here on this map of the oceans everything is reversed—
the land all black except for the names of the continents
whereas the watery parts, colored blue,
have topographical features and even place names

like the Bermuda Rise, which sounds harmless enough
as does the Cocos Ridge, but how about exploring
The Guafo Fracture Zone when you're all alone?
And from the many plateaus and seamounts—

the Falkland, the Manning, the Azores—
all you could see is water and if you're lucky
a big fish swallowing a school of smaller ones
through the bars of your deep-sea diver's helmet.

And talk about depth: at 4,000 feet below the surface,
where you love to float on your back all summer,
we enter the Midnight Zone where the monkfish
quietly says his prayers in order to attract fresh prey,

and drop another couple of miles and you
have reached The Abyss where the sea cucumber
is said to undulate minding its own business
unless it's deceiving an attacker with its luminescence

before disappearing into the blackness.
What attacker, I can hear you asking,
could be down there messing with the sea cucumber?
and that is exactly why I crumpled the map into a ball

and stuffed it in a metal wastebasket
before heading out for a long walk along a sunny trail
in the thin, high-desert air, accompanied
by juniper trees, wildflowers, and that gorgeous hawk.

Biographical Notes in an Anthology of Haiku

Walking the dog,
you meet
lots of dogs.

— Sōshi

One was a seventeenth-century doctor
arrested for trading with Dutch merchants.
One loved *sake* then disappeared
through the doors of a monastery in his final years.

Another was a freight agent
who became a nun after her husband died.
Quite a few lived the samurai life
excelling in the lance, sword, and horseback riding

as well as poetry, painting, and calligraphy.
This one started writing poems at eight,
and that one was a rice merchant of some repute.
One was a farmer, another ran a pharmacy.

But next to the name of my favorite, Sōshi,
there is no information at all,
not even a guess at his years and a question mark,
which left me looking vacantly at the wall

after I had read his perfect little poem.
Whether you poke your nose into Plato
or get serious with St. John of the Cross,
you will not find a more unassailable truth

than walking the dog, you meet lots of dogs
or a sweeter one, I would add.
If I were a teacher with a student
who deserved punishment, I would make him write

Walking the dog, you meet lots of dogs
on the blackboard a hundred thousand times
or until the boy discovered
that this was no punishment at all, but a treat.

And if I were that student
holding a broken piece of chalk
ready to begin filling the panels of the board,
I would first stand by one of the tall windows

to watch the other students running in the yard
shouting each other's names,
the large autumn trees sheltering their play,
everything so obvious now, thanks to the genius of Sōshi.

Florida in December

From this dock by a lake
where I walked down after a late dinner—

some clouds blown like gauze across the stars,
and every so often an airplane
crossing the view from left to right,
its green starboard wing light
descending against this soft wind into the city airport.

The permanent stars,
I think on the walk back to the house,
and the momentary clouds in their vaporous shapes,
I go on, my hands clasped behind my back
like a professor of nothing in particular.

Then I am near enough to the house—
warm, amber windows,
cold dots of lights from the Christmas tree,

glad to have seen those clouds, now blown away,
happy to be under the stars,
constant and swirling in the firmament,
and here on the threshold of this house
with all its work and hope,
and steady enough under a fixed and shifting sky.

Dining Alone

I would rather eat at the bar,
but such behavior is regarded
by professionals as a form of denial,
so here I am seated alone
at a table with a white tablecloth
attended by an elderly waiter with no name—
ideal conditions for dining alone
according to the connoisseurs of this minor talent.

I have brought neither book nor newspaper
since reading material is considered cheating.
Eating alone, they say, means eating alone
not in the company of Montaigne
or the ever-engaging Nancy Mitford.

Nor do I keep glancing up as if waiting
for someone who inevitably fails to appear—
a sign of moral weakness
to those who take this practice seriously.

And the rewards?
I am thinking of an obvious one right now
as I take the time to contemplate
on my lifted fork a piece of trout with almond slices.

And I can enjoy swirling the wine in my glass
until it resembles a whirlpool
in a 19th-century painting of a ship foundering in a storm.

Then there are the looks of envy
from that fellow on the blind date
and the long-married couple facing each other in silence.

I pierced a buttered spear of asparagus
and wondered if the moon would be visible tonight,
but uncapping my pen was out of the question
for writing, too, is frowned upon
by the true champions of solitude.

All that would have to wait
until after I have walked home,
collar up, under the streetlights.
Not until I would hear the echo of the front door
closing behind me could I record
in a marbled notebook—
like the ones I had as a schoolboy—
my observations about the art
of dining alone in the company of strangers.

Lucky Bastards

From the deck of the swimming pool
you could see the planes taking off from LAX
and whenever my father visited his friend there,
the two of them would sit in the sun with their drinks

and kill the time between golf and dinner
by betting on whether the next plane would bank
left or right, and if you picked the long shot—
one continuing straight over the ocean—you got double.

The time I was there with them, I watched
the singles and fives changing hands
as they laughed "You lucky bastard!"
and I learned again the linkage between friendship and money

and the sweet primacy of one over the other,
which is not to say that Sandburg's six-volume
biography of Lincoln or the writings of Lao Tzu
are not also excellent teachers, each in its own way.

"I Love You"

Early on, I noticed that you always say it
to each of your children
as you are getting off the phone with them
just as you never fail to say it
to me whenever we arrive at the end of a call.

It's all new to this only child.
I never heard my parents say it,
at least not on such a regular basis,
nor did it ever occur to me to miss it.
To say I love you pretty much every day

would have seemed strangely obvious,
like saying I'm looking at you
when you are standing there looking at someone.
If my parents had started saying it
a lot, I would have started to worry about them.

Of course, I always like hearing it from you.
That is never a cause for concern.
The problem is I now find myself saying it back
if only because just saying good-bye
then hanging up would make me seem discourteous.

But like Bartleby, I would prefer not to
say it so often, would prefer instead to save it
for special occasions, like shouting it out as I leaped
into the red mouth of a volcano
with you standing helplessly on the smoking rim,

or while we are desperately clasping hands
before our plane plunges into the Gulf of Mexico,
which are only two of the examples I had in mind,
but enough, as it turns out, to make me
want to say it to you right now,

and what better place than in the final couplet
of a poem where, as every student knows, it really counts.

Unholy Sonnet #1

Death, one thing you can be proud of
is all the room you manage to take up
in this *Concordance to the Poems of John Donne*,
edited by Homer Carroll Combs and published in 1945.

Mighty and dreadful are your tall columns here,
(though *soul* and *love* put you in deep shade)
for you outnumber *man* and outscore even *life* itself,
and you are roughly tied with *God* and, strangely, *eyes*.

But no one likes the way you swell,
not even in these scholarly rows,
where from the complex fields of his poems
each word has returned to the alphabet with a sigh.

And lovelier than you are the ones that only once he tried:
syllable and *porcelain*, but also *beach, cup, snail, lamp,* and *pie*.

If This Were a Job I'd Be Fired

When you wake up with nothing,
but you are nonetheless drawn to your sunny chair
near the French doors, it may be necessary
to turn to some of the others to get you going.

So I opened a book of Gerald Stern
but I didn't want to face my age
by writing about my childhood in the 1940s.
Then I read two little Merwins

which made me feel I should apply
for a position in a corner sandwich shop.
And it only took one Simic,
which ended with a couple on a rooftop

watching a child on fire leap from a window,
to get me to replace the cap on my pen,
put on some sweatpants and go for a walk
around the lake to think of a new career,

but not before I told you all about it
in well, look at this, five quatrains—
better than nothing for a weekday,
I thought, as I headed merrily out the door.

Friends in the Dark

Signs and countersigns should be established
to determine your friends in the dark.

—Robert Rogers, *Rules for Ranging*

Such a ripe opportunity is presented here
to expand what Rogers meant,
making those friends our own friends and the dark, The Dark.

But is there not enough in this early manual
on guerrilla warfare written in 1758
in the midst of the French and Indian War

and still in use to this day
by those who must cross on foot
the unfriendly fields and woods of combat?

Yes, given the common guile of the world, we might
send one or two men forward to scout
the area and avoid traps before breaking camp.

And as far as being attacked from the rear goes,
sure, *immediately reverse order,*
and the same goes if attacked from the flank

as we often are, blindsided by a friend
in the dark or right in the face
outside a motel in the glow of a drink machine.

But why not honor the literal for a change,
let the rules speak for themselves,
and not get all periwinkle with allegory?

In the light of rule #20—
avoid passing lakes too close to the edge
as the enemy could trap you against the water's edge—

could we not stop to absorb
the plight of these hungry rangers
lost in the wilds up and down the Canadian border,

wind rustling the maples, the scent of rain
and danger, and no one having a clue
that their fighting would one day be written down?

Avoid regular river fords
as these are often watched by the enemy,
may make us think of the times we have been wounded

by an arrow while wading through life,
but tonight let's just heed the rules of Rogers
and look for a better place to cross a river.

No, not the river of life,
a real river, the one we cannot see
there is so much to hack through to get to its bank.

Flying Over West Texas at Christmas

Oh, little town far below
with a ruler line of a road running through you,
you anonymous cluster of houses and barns,
miniaturized by this altitude
in a land as parched as Bethlehem
might have been somewhere around the year zero—

a beautiful song should be written about you
which choirs could sing in their lofts
and carolers standing in a semicircle
could carol in front of houses topped with snow.

For surely some admirable person was born
within the waffle-iron grid of your streets,
who then went on to perform some small miracles,
placing a hand on the head of a child
or shaking a cigarette out of the pack for a stranger.

But maybe it is best not to compose a hymn
or chisel into tablets the code of his behavior
or convene a tribunal of men in robes to explain his words.

Let us not press the gold leaf of his name
onto a page of vellum or hang his image from a nail.

Better to fly over this little town with nothing
but the hope that someone visits his grave

once a year, pushing open the low iron gate
then making her way toward him
through the rows of the others
before bending to prop up some flowers before the stone.

Last Meal

The waiter was dressed in black
and wore a hood,
and when we pleaded for a little more time,
he raised his pencil over his order pad.

And later when he came back
to ask if we were finished,
we shook our heads no,
our forks trembling over our empty plates.

A Word About Transitions

Moreover is not a good way to begin a poem
though many start somewhere in the middle.

Secondly should not be placed
at the opening of your second stanza.

Furthermore should be regarded
as a word to avoid,

Aforementioned is rarely found
in poems at all and for good reason.

Most steer clear of *notwithstanding*
and the same goes for

nevertheless, however,
as a consequence, in any event,

subsequently,
and *as we have seen in the previous chapters.*

Finally's appearance at the top
of the final stanza is not going to help.

All of which suggests (another no-no)
that poems don't need to tell us where we are

or what is soon to come.
For example, the white bowl of lemons

on a table by a window
is fine all by itself

and, *in conclusion,* so are
seven elephants standing in the rain.

The Names

(for the victims of September 11th
and their survivors)

Yesterday, I lay awake in the palm of the night.
A fine rain stole in, unhelped by any breeze,
And when I saw the silver glaze on the windows,
I started with A, with Ackerman, as it happened,
Then Baxter and Calabro,
Davis and Eberling, names falling into place
As droplets fell through the dark.
Names printed on the ceiling of the night.
Names slipping around a watery bend.
Twenty-six willows on the banks of a stream.

In the morning, I walked out barefoot
Among thousands of flowers
Heavy with dew like the eyes of tears,
And each had a name—
Fiori inscribed on a yellow petal
Then Gonzalez and Han, Ishikawa and Jenkins.

Names written in the air
And stitched into the cloth of the day.
A name under a photograph taped to a mailbox.

Monogram on a torn shirt,
I see you spelled out on storefront windows
And on the bright unfurled awnings of this city.
I say the syllables as I turn a corner—
Kelly and Lee,
Medina, Nardella, and O'Connor.

When I peer into the woods,
I see a thick tangle where letters are hidden
As in a puzzle concocted for children.
Parker and Quigley in the twigs of an ash,
Rizzo, Schubert, Torres, and Upton,
Secrets in the boughs of an ancient maple.

Names written in the pale sky.
Names rising in the updraft amid buildings.
Names silent in stone
Or cried out behind a door.
Names blown over the earth and out to sea.

In the evening—weakening light, the last swallows.
A boy on a lake lifts his oars.
A woman by a window puts a match to a candle,
And the names are outlined on the rose clouds—
Vanacore and Wallace,
(let X stand, if it can, for the ones unfound)
Then Young and Ziminsky, the final jolt of Z.

Names etched on the head of a pin.
One name spanning a bridge, another undergoing a tunnel.
A blue name needled into the skin.
Names of citizens, workers, mothers and fathers,
The bright-eyed daughter, the quick son.
Alphabet of names in green rows in a field.
Names in the small tracks of birds.
Names lifted from a hat
Or balanced on the tip of the tongue.
Names wheeled into the dim warehouse of memory.
So many names, there is barely room on the walls of the heart.

ACKNOWLEDGMENTS

The author is grateful to the editors of the following periodicals where some of these poems first appeared:

American Arts Quarterly: "Carrara"

The Atlantic: "Orient," "Osprey"

Barnes and Noble Review: "Note to Antonín Dvořák"

Boulevard: "After the Funeral," "Elusive," "Here and There"

The Cortland Review: "Lines Written in a Garden in Herefordshire"

Ecotone: "Best Fall"

Five Points: "To My Favorite 17-Year-Old High School Girl"

The Georgia Review: "Drinking Alone"

The Gettysburg Review: "The Music of the Spheres," "Villanelle"

Harper's: "The Sandhill Cranes of Nebraska"

New Ohio Review: "All Eyes," "The Suggestion Box"

The New York Times: "The Names"

The New Yorker: "Catholicism"

Poetry: "Cheerios," "Irish Poetry," "Report from the Subtropics"

A Public Space: "Lincoln"

Raritan: "Unholy Sonnet #1," "Biographical Notes on the Haiku Poets"

Shenandoah: "Sunday Walk"

Slate: "Foundling"

Smithsonian Magazine: "The Deep," "The Unfortunate Traveler"

The Southampton Review: "Foundling," "Flying Over West Texas at Christmas," "Heraclitus on Vacation," "Lines Written at Flying Point Beach," "Looking for a Friend in a Crowd of Arriving Passengers," "Lucky Bastards"

Southern Poetry Review: "Promenade"

The Times Literary Supplement: "Last Meal"

Tin House: "A Word About Transitions"

"Foundling" was selected by Denise Duhamel for
    The Best American Poetry 2013

"Here and There" was selected by Kevin Young for
The Best American Poetry 2011

"Unholy Sonnet #1" was reprinted in *Harper's*

The translation of the Hadrian epigraph is by W. S. Merwin
and appeared in *Poetry* and in *The Shadow of Sirius*.

For her help with many aspects of this book's coming into being,
my gratitude to Suzannah Gilman.

About the Author

BILLY COLLINS is the author of ten collections of poetry, including *Horoscopes for the Dead, Ballistics, The Trouble with Poetry and Other Poems, Nine Horses, Sailing Alone Around the Room, Questions About Angels, The Apple That Astonished Paris, The Art of Drowning,* and *Picnic, Lightning*. He is also the editor of *Poetry 180: A Turning Back to Poetry, 180 More: Extraordinary Poems for Every Day,* and *Bright Wings: An Illustrated Anthology of Poems About Birds.* A distinguished professor of English at Lehman College of the City University of New York and a distinguished Fellow at the Winter Park Institute of Rollins College, he was Poet Laureate of the United States from 2001 to 2003 and Poet Laureate of New York State from 2004 to 2006. He divides his time between New York and Florida, and speaks regularly around the country and the world.

About the Type

The text of this book was set in Filosofia. It was designed in 1996 by Zuzana Licko, who created it for digital typesetting as an interpretation of the sixteenth-century typeface Bodoni. Filosofia, an example of Licko's unusual font designs, has classical proportions with a strong vertical feeling, softened by rounded droplike serifs. She has designed many typefaces and is the cofounder of *Emigre* magazine, where many of them first appeared. Born in Bratislava, Czechoslovakia, Licko came to the United States in 1968. She studied graphic communications at the University of California at Berkeley, graduating in 1984.